Project Management Institute

Managing Stakeholders as Clients
as Clients
Sponsorship, Partnership, Leadership, and Citizenship

Mário Henrique Trentim, PMI-RMP, PMP

Library of Congress Cataloging-in-Publication Data

Trentim, Mário Henrique.
  Managing stakeholders as clients : sponsorship, partnership, leadership, and citizenship /
Mário Henrique Trentim.
      p. cm.
  Includes bibliographical references.
  ISBN 978-1-935589-65-5 (pbk. : alk. paper) 1. Project management. 2. Customer relations.
I. Title.
  HD69.P75T74 2013
  658.4'04--dc23
                          2012046110

ISBN: 978-1-935589-65-5

Published by: Project Management Institute, Inc.
                   14 Campus Boulevard
                   Newtown Square, Pennsylvania 19073-3299 USA
                   Phone: +610-356-4600
                   Fax: +610-356-4647
                   Email: customercare@pmi.org
                   Internet: www.PMI.org

PMI Publications welcomes corrections and comments on its books. Please feel free to send
comments on typographical, formatting, or other errors. Simply make a copy of the relevant page
of the book, mark the error, and send it to: Book Editor, PMI Publications, 14 Campus Boulevard,
Newtown Square, PA 19073-3299 USA.

To inquire about discounts for resale or educational purposes, please contact the PMI Book
Service Center.
        PMI Book Service Center
        P.O. Box 932683, Atlanta, GA 31193-2683 USA
        Phone: 1-866-276-4764 (within the U.S. or Canada) or +1-770-280-4129 (globally)
        Fax: +1-770-280-4113
        Email: info@bookorders.pmi.org

10 9 8 7 6 5 4 3 2

To Stefânia, Pietra, and Maysa with love.

Acknowledgments

I would like to thank Project Management Institute (PMI) for the opportunity to publish this book. I would also like to thank PMI and its Chapters for all the volunteer opportunities that helped me and many others to develop ourselves in project management.

I have to say a special thank you to Ashley Richardson, Barbara Walsh and Dan Goldfischer, great professionals who helped me in reviewing and editing my drafts to turn them into this book.

Professors Issam Ghazzawi, PhD, and Darli Rodrigues Vieira, PhD, contributed with valuable information and advices. I have no words to thank them.

In large and intricate projects, I believe that we have to manage stakeholders as clients using the approach of complex sales.

For those of you who don't know anything about sales and marketing, learn it. You'll need more than technical skills in projects, as you know.

Selling used cars is very different from selling aircraft or enterprise resource management software. In small sales, the customer usually focuses on price. The seller must quickly close a sale. Once the customer buys a product, the relationship between him and the seller typically ends. In large complex sales, this is very different.

First, in complex sales, you take a lot of time to achieve your goal. The buyer frequently doesn't know what he really wants, and he isn't able compare alternatives offered. Second, big sales involve strategic decisions. So, they have great impact in the long run. Big sales are also very expensive for the buyer. Finally, you must build confidence and create a long relationship between you (seller) and the buyer before and after closing the sale. Does this sound familiar to you as a project manager?

In big and multifaceted projects, we deal not only with a lot of stakeholders but also with expectations, politics, technical decisions, and with more. My approach to these types of projects involves four basic aspects: sponsorship, partnership, leadership, and citizenship. I call them fondly "the four ships." If you know how to navigate these "ships," they may bring you home safely. However, they may take you to hell if you don't know how to manage them.

Sponsorship is the basis of a project. And you, as a project manager, have to keep your sponsors interested, involved, and supportive. Partnership is a broad concept or aspect in project management. You'll have to deal with clients, contractors, and partnerships of all types. You are a project manager not superman, so you'll probably need help to finish the project, right? Keep in mind that good and competent people are the most valuable (and rare) asset in the world. If you lead them well, they may be extremely creative and hard-working, even in tough situations. Your team can make miracles happen if you know how to guide, motivate, and care for them. Leadership is another important aspect in project management. Finally, the last but not least important aspect is citizenship. Every project should add value. Citizenship is about sustainability and responsibility. Actually, it's more than this. Citizenship includes values and morality that should drive our efforts as project managers not only because we have a code of conduct but also because ethics must lie in our hearts. In the end, your reputation and conscience are the most valuable assets you can have.

It is an honor and a pleasure to share these ideas with you—the reader.

Foreword

Adding Value and Organizational Success Through the Power of Stakeholder Management

Why do some organizations grow, succeed, and thrive while other, once-powerful organizations do not survive the test of time? One simple explanation for organizational success has to do with how well these organizations are able to manage its stakeholders. In today's global economy, managers can no longer rely on brands, logos, revenues, and margins to sustain their organizations. They are compelled to focus on meeting their stakeholders' needs and expectations, including the commitment to their employees' needs and satisfaction'; commitment to the environment and society (social and philanthropic responsibilities); commitment to their shareholders and to the organizational growth (economic responsibilities); and the commitment to their legal and ethical obligations.

Managing stakeholder interests has been the central focus of my role as a former executive and a current university professor. I have been an avid advocate of employees' commitment and employee well-being, as it is crucial to organizational sustainability and success. When a talented employee leaves, an organization loses not only a valuable employee but also the accumulated knowledge associated with the core capabilities and competencies the organization depends on. Fortunately, in his book Managing Stakeholders as Clients, author Mario Henrique Trentim has discovered, through his passionate, hands-on management and complex project sales, his own method of stakeholders' management, which is deftly applied in his book. Mario defines the stakeholder approach as achieving a balance of interests among the various parties internal and external to any organization.

Mario masterfully illustrates his approach to difficult projects using a "four ships" metaphor. These ships are: (1) sponsorship, (2) partnership, (3) leadership, and (4) citizenship. He states that you can come home safely if you know how to navigate these ships. However, he cautions that if you do not know how to balance them, you will be heading into the unknown. Case-in point is that each of the stakeholders (or stakeholder groups) controls important resources that are valued in any organization. Hence, an organization is only effective if it is capable of satisfying the interests of the groups controlling such resources.

This is a well-researched and rich guide based on the author's use of personal reflection about his experiences in working and teaching project management for many years. This book will be helpful to many individuals regardless of their position in the organization. This engaging and elegantly written synthesis of stakeholder management has a comprehensive approach to managing projects, especially tricky ones.

Issam A. Ghazzaw, PhD
Associate Professor of Management
College of Business and Public Management
University of La Verne, California, USA

If you were asked, "What is a project manager's main role?"
what would you say? The answer is to perform integration
management to put all the pieces of a project together
into a cohesive whole.

Rita Mulcahy

Contents

By Darli Vieira PhD, Université Du Québec

Introduction

By Darli Vieira PhD, Université du Québec

Stakeholder Management: A rationale, step-wise approach and toolkit of best practices. That's what you are going to find in this book.

Instead of just reading books and taking courses on how to recover failed projects, executives and project managers should invest in stakeholder management in order to prevent failure. Everybody says that project management has to be proactive, but commonly we face reactive patterns in organizations. Due to time and cost pressures, we lose focus on building value to organizations through clients.

If you ever asked "why are we doing this project?" probably that is because you don't know who your stakeholders are. When you know your stakeholders, the objectives of your project become clear as a result of stakeholders' requirements and expectations. So, if you manage large and intricate projects, if you want to make a difference through successful project management, then you should read this book.

Modern stakeholder management tried to explain, apply and extend Freeman's Stakeholder Theory. One of the biggest problems faced by executives, project managers and other professionals who deal with stakeholders is that there are few directions about how to manage stakeholders in practice. There are plenty of books and articles mentioning stakeholder management, but it is less frequent to find case studies and guides about stakeholder management.

As a result, project managers don't know how to manage stakeholders. Although everyone knows the importance of stakeholders and stakeholder management, the problem starts with stakeholder identification. Most of the project managers don't know how to identify stakeholders properly; they simply use half-baked recipes and templates. Generic approaches such as brainstorming are helpful but not sufficient to identify stakeholders. Poor stakeholder identification results in lots of forgotten stakeholders who may even paralyze or kill the project.

Stakeholder analysis is useless if you did poor stakeholder identification. Analysis will be incomplete also. Strategies to manage or engage stakeholders will be flawed and your project may end up in trouble just because of negligence in stakeholder management.

In this book, Mario brings us a great combination of theory and practice. You will have the privilege to find in one book academic knowledge and research allied to pragmatic and real applications of stakeholder management in large and intricate projects. Comparing Stakeholder Theory with the approaches of the *PMBOK® Guide* and PRINCE2, Mario goes beyond and unveils step-by-step procedures to identify stakeholders, analyze stakeholders and engage stakeholders.

Considering that we cannot manage stakeholders' expectations, Mario proposes an action research approach, based on Checkland's SSM, where the project's scope is built with the help of stakeholders. Key stakeholders are involved and engaged from the beginning until the end of the project in a collaborative way. Of course, there are negative stakeholders, or project's enemies, that project managers have to deal with. And Mario shows tools and techniques to conquer and to manage them.

In its core, *Managing Stakeholders as Clients* stands up for a rational analogy between complex sales and project management. Mario intelligently states and shows that every stakeholder can and should be treated as a client.

Darli Rodrigues Vieira, PhD
Professor
Université du Québec
à Trois-Rivières, Canada

Chapter 1

Foundations

An organization is a social structure of various stakeholders
who all want to satisfy their own goals through interaction.

Jurgen Appelo

1.1 Beyond Traditional Project Management

Intrigued by the complex sales approach, I had an insight after talking with a CEO. While talking, I couldn't help noticing his stacks of books about engineering, sales, and marketing. The curious part is that he is CEO of a big, multinational engineering company.

This CEO, an engineer with PhD degree and strong technical knowledge and experience, built a great career and reputation. This grabbed my attention. Why would a rocket scientist have so many books about sales and marketing? The products and services of his company are intricate and expensive. It builds incredible large systems with on-the-edge technology. For this reason, he needs to know a lot about complex sales to close a deal.

We need a new approach to manage intricate and large projects because stakeholders are much more important in these projects than in small projects. Why? Because large, intricate projects involve strategic decisions, conflicting requirements and expectations, and many other hidden aspects.

1.2 A Word of Caution

I assume that the readers of this book have some knowledge about project management. We are going to use *A Guide to the Project Management Body of Knowledge (PMBOK® Guide)* (Project Management Institute, 2008) as a reference, and I advise you to look at it, if you don't know it yet.

We are going to talk about stakeholder management and its influence on other project areas. Stakeholders are entities that will benefit or suffer from the project's results directly or indirectly. When I say entities, I mean people, groups, institutions, or any other kind of subject that can affect or be affected by the project.

As project managers, we will have to deal with stakeholders. We will depend on some of them also using stakeholder management.

Customers and users, for example, are an important source of requirements that will influence the project scope definition. If you already know something about project management, you will agree that *scope* is the only important area *by the end of the project.*

All other knowledge areas (integration, time, cost, quality, human resources, communications, risks, and acquisitions) will support and help the project manager and team to achieve the desired result: scope. In the end, stakeholders will be happy (or not) with what you are going to deliver them (product, service, and other deliverables). Your client will not want reports, schedules, and plans. The client wants the product, service, or unique result that your project was meant to deliver, right? Everything else is to support and to assure that you are progressing toward the goal.

Scope is the basis of projects and project management. We first collect requirements, and then we define scope and all other areas that depend on scope. From the work breakdown structure (WBS), we will define activities that will be the basis for resources estimation. Therefore, schedule and budget depend on the scope. Quality will also depend on scope and requirements. Human resource needs are related to the activities that depend on deliverables and scope. Acquisitions are directly dependent on scope and deliverables. Finally, communications will support the whole project, while risks also depend much on scope and deliverables.

Considering that scope is to satisfy stakeholders, I state with confidence that scope management and stakeholder management are the basis of project management. However, these two very important areas are often mistreated. We are always in a hurry, so we superficially communicate with stakeholders, quickly define scope, and then focus on project management processes related to time and cost.

In the middle of the project, during execution, we encounter scope problems and use project management tools and techniques like fast tracking and crashing. And we feel that we are good project managers because we make the effort, and in the end, we deliver project results with some efficacy.

1.3 Management Is Overrated!

Saying that management is overrated may seem a little strange. After all, isn't this book about management? Stakeholder management? Scope management? Project management? Yes, but nowadays, and incorrectly I think, many consider that management tools and skills can solve all the problems. Frequently, we forget to foster and grow technical skills, knowledge, and competence. Everybody wants to be a manager because managers earn more money than technicians, technologists, and engineers. Or do they? There are many project managers who earn less than the people they manage. Why? Because in the end, we want scope, meaning results. And without experts, technicians, technologists, and engineers or any other kind of specialist, we won't have it! You won't build a space shuttle without technical knowledge; it doesn't matter how many managers you have or how good they may be.

Each of us must develop soft skills and management skills, but we can't forget our core business: technical aspects of your profession. If you are managing marketing projects, organizational projects, mergers and acquisitions, product development projects, engineering projects, or any other kind of project, you have to know something about the subject. You must know what it takes to complete the project, its goals, and what you need to understand the big picture. No management of soft skills will save you from failure if you don't understand the technical aspects, the requirements, and some of the how-to of your project.

To be a good manager, you must know what you're talking about.

Talent is also overrated. We tend to believe that some skills are intrinsic, either you are born with them or not. This is not true. We can develop any ability if we dedicate the right attention and amount of time. This is called "deliberate practice" (Gladwell, 2007). You don't really need talent. You need persistence, focus and discipline to achieve consistency and success.

Another paradigm is that a few big stars could do the job. The problem with stars is that they achieve excellent results only when they want, and they may leave your team or your company when you need them. What we really need is a group of people working hard together. Actually, as a project manager, we must foster and grow high-performance teams, as we will see later in this book. Building high-performance teams is difficult, and it takes time and effort. However, if you are like the majority of project managers, you frequently forget that your team members are stakeholders.

I have mentioned "the four ships." If you don't have a good sponsor to support you with authority and resources (sponsorship), if you don't treat your stakeholders as partners (partnership), if you don't know how to lead and protect your team (leadership), and if you don't live by your values (citizenship), you'll probably fail your project. Or you might be very lucky if you have any success.

1.4 Hot Topics in Project Management

Times have changed. Projects are getting more complex. When I see the CHAOS Reports[1], I wonder why we are not getting better as project managers. Project management has evolved a lot in the past 10 years. If we are not having better results in the same pace, maybe that's because the projects that we manage are getting more intricate and large. We are facing different challenges as project managers, and we must change the way we manage projects to cope with them.

---

[1]CHAOS Knowledge Center. The Standish Group. Accessed on July 20th 2012, www.blog.standishgroup.pmresearch.

While I was writing this book, Project Management Institute (PMI) and the International Council of Systems Engineering (INCOSE) reached an agreement to work together[2] to help organizations improve program and project success. And, in my opinion, this is a step toward the solution of the problems that I introduced in the Acknowledgments of this book.

Management is overrated. And, partly because many professionals are focusing only on project management processes, while forgetting product-oriented processes. INCOSE's approach, on the other hand, has a more technical view, mainly when it concerns systems engineering and requirements management. Actually, I could say that systems engineering is all about stakeholders and their requirements.

You don't have to focus on the "engineering" part. When you start a project to change your organization's structure, for example, you will benefit from systems and requirements engineering processes. Every project has goals and requirements, and we could represent almost every solution as a system.

Many projects fail because they lack clear objectives and requirements. Other projects have unrealistic goals and requirements that cannot be achieved or measured. These problems lead us to stakeholder management, expectations, and requirements identification.

Reviewing hot topics on project management, we are always faced with *risks* and *stakeholders*. We could say we have a strong knowledge about other knowledge areas such as time, cost, quality, and acquisitions. Our weak point is often related to people, human resources, communications, and expectations management.

Risk management is a competitive advantage in today's world due partly to increasing complexity and enormous new challenges. Risks and stakeholders are two interrelated topics. For now, just bear in mind that your relationship with stakeholders will (or will not) help you lower your risks, even risks not related to the stakeholders (technical or economic risks, for example) because they will help you overcome the problems.

The mention of stakeholders segues into other hot topics in project management: customer satisfaction and project success. You can also call it scope management and change management. If you've already seen a never-ending nightmare project, you know what these words means.

Sometimes, I see project managers complaining about their stakeholders. They say, "stakeholder X always changes his mind" or "stakeholder Y creates obstacles to my project," and so on. Wake up! Stakeholders are not a problem. If there is any problem, the problem is you, the project manager, and your project.

---

[2]PMI and INCOSE Align To Help Organizations Improve Program Success. International Council of Systems Engineering. Accessed on June 11st 2012, www.incose.org/newsevents/news/details .aspx?id=237.

Project managers may react adversely to hearing that they and their project are the problem with anger. But they don't get angry with me. Imagine that you are a stakeholder, any stakeholder: user, client, functional manager, contractors, government, etc. As a project manager, your project is a *temporary* endeavor to create *a unique result*. So, your project will create something that didn't exist before, something that wasn't there. You're annoying your stakeholders' peace! You're possibly shaking their worlds, their zone of comfort.

As a functional manager, for example, I will have to give up my status quo. I would be "forced" by your project to learn how to use the new enterprise resource planning (ERP) system that you want to install! Do you really think I would help you? Is the functional manager the problem? No.

You, as a project manager, and your project are going to change the environment. Your team will produce some result, and as a project manager, your job is to convince stakeholders that they are going to benefit from the outcome. Show them what they will earn! If you fail, they won't help. And as long as your stakeholders are not happy, your project is doomed to failure.

So, project managers have to understand, influence, communicate, and persuade.[3] This is why I use the complex sales approach in intricate projects. We will see the best practices in stakeholder management.

1.5 Best Practices

We now have to deal with many more stakeholders than we did in the past. Moreover, these "new" stakeholders are much more demanding! Consequently, to manage big and intricate projects, you need a different approach.[4]

Before diving into our approach of stakeholders as clients, I would like to be sure that we have some common ground. In the following, we have the stakeholders' management processes according to the *PMBOK® Guide*—Fourth Edition (Project Management Institute, 2008). Stakeholders' identification and management of their expectations are included in the Project Communications Management Knowledge Area (Project Management Institute, 2008, ch. 10).

We know that stakeholders are those folks (or organizations) with a vested interest in your project. They will affect or be affected by your project, directly or indirectly.

Although it's difficult to measure project success, we could say that a project is successful when it achieves its objectives and meets or exceeds the expectations

---

[3]If you didn't read Sun Tzu, hurry. Read Machiavelli also. But remember that in project management it's always better to create allies and turn enemies into allies than fight against enemies. When we talk about hidden stakeholders, you'll understand this point.

[4]You should also read Daniel Goleman. Project management, as any other kind of management, is more about people, politics, expectations, and emotional intelligence than about anything else.

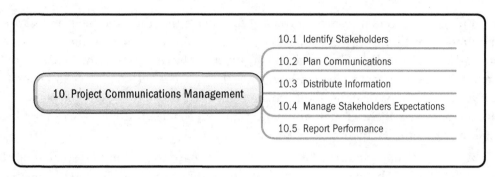

Figure 1-1: Communications management processes.

of the stakeholders. Hartman (2000) said that success means happy stakeholders. Even if all the deliverables are met and the objectives are satisfied, if your key stakeholders aren't happy, nobody is happy.

Consequently, to be successful, the first step is identify stakeholders in the beginning of the project. Stakeholder identification is not a one-time process. You should continue to ask fellow team members and stakeholders if there are other stakeholders who should be a part of the project. As we identify stakeholders, we can develop strategies to manage their expectations.

During project execution, we'll deal with stakeholders every day. Therefore, communication skills are an indispensable tool for project managers. Some say that a project manager spends around 90 percent of his or her time communicating. If this communication is not effective, it's a useless waste of energy.

We also have to consider that there are some processes related to stakeholders in Project Human Resources Management (Project Management Institute, ch. 9). The project team and its members individually are a special category of stakeholders.

As a project manager, you'll have to build, guide, and protect your team members. And, of course, you'll have to help them solve personal and professional conflicts now and then.

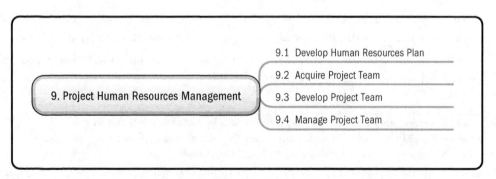

Figure 1-2: Human resources management.

We'll discuss the processes, tools, and techniques described in the *A Guide to the Project Management Body of Knowledge (PMBOK® Guide)* in detail later in this book. For now, I would like to introduce agile project management methods. Project Management Institute recently launched a new certification program, PMI Agile Certified Practioner (PMI-ACP)®, recognizing the benefits and importance of agile project management.

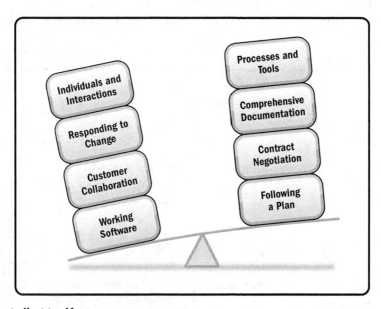

Figure 1-3: Agile Manifesto.

For me, one of the biggest contributions of agile is its focus on people. Another important aspect is that plans can be changed. In addition, a third interesting factor is that we can start working to be able to start working.

Sometimes, people think that we must plan every detail before executing the project, which is not feasible for multifaceted projects. We are now building innovation and it's hard to plan all the details in advance! We get to know more about the product as we move on in the project. This is something like the rolling wave planning with a positive feedback: plan, build, learn, re-plan, re-build, and so on.

Those who say that agile doesn't use documents don't know what they are talking about. Those who preach that agile is only for small IT projects are also wrong. Agile is scalable, and it is compatible with the approach of the *PMBOK® Guide*.

Actually, management has to fit the project. Project managers soon realize that different approaches are used contingent on each project's characteristics. Shenhar and Dvir (2007), for example, proposed the "Diamond Framework," also known as the NCTP model, which considers four dimensions of a project:

1. "Novelty" – How intensely new are crucial aspects of the project?
2. "Technology" – Where does the project exist on the scale from low-tech to super high-tech?
3. "Complexity" – How complicated are the product, the process, and the project?
4. "Pace" – How urgent is the work? Is the timing "normal, fast, time-critical or blitz"?

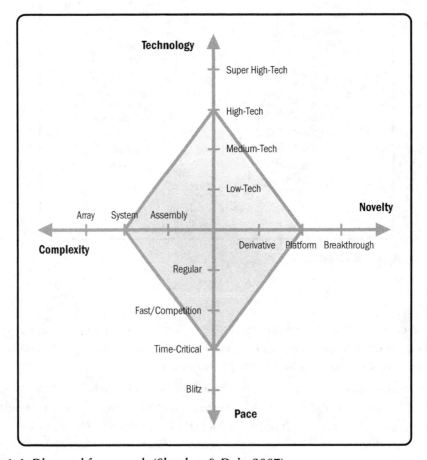

Figure 1-4: Diamond framework (Shenhar & Dvir, 2007).

Considering we have a large spectrum of projects with different characteristics and complexity, it's obvious that we need a great repertory of project management methodologies. That's why a good project manager must have a toolbox with processes, tools, and techniques from different "manufacturers" or "suppliers" (PMI,

OGC, ISO, IPMA, Scrum Alliance, standardization organizations, proprietary methodologies, etc.).

Although every project is unique, we can find quite a number of common features in a wide range of projects (Shenhar & Dvir, 2007), which allows us to devise better management practices tailored to fit "categories" or types of projects.

Throughout this book, we will mention theories and best practices in project management to help us build our contingent approach to project management focused on the stakeholders' theory (Freeman, 1984). We take the *PMBOK® Guide* as a reference, but we will get back to agile when we talk about scope definition and management and when we talk about the team in Chapters 7 and 11. We will also study the *PRINCE2™* (OGC, 2009) methodology in Chapters 4, 6, and 10.

1.6 Stakeholders as Clients

In the past, organizations did not have to worry so much about stakeholder management because power was concentrated in their hands. Stakeholders, most of the time, did not know how they would be affected by the outcomes nor did they have interest in the projects carried on by organizations. However, in this shared-power world, no one is fully in charge; no organization "contains" the problem (Kettl, 2002; quoted in Bryson, 2003).

The world is faster, globalized, and more competitive, which creates big pressure to innovate and be the first movers. Consequently, as projects are getting larger and more intricate due to the increase in complexity of problems and opportunities faced by organizations, more stakeholders are involved or affected.

But, and that's a big but, time to market *might be useless*. Timing *does not guarantee success*. What? Am I saying that the right time might not be right? Yes. Success is time to market *with the right product*—not only time but also timing *with the right solution*. Of course, we want the right solution. However, research shows us that half of the projects result in useless outcomes[5]. In the end, the stakeholders are not happy, they do not need the result of the project anymore or its outcome does not satisfy their needs.

Then, what's wrong? We don't understand (or we don't dedicate enough effort to understand) the underlying problem that the project outcome must solve. And this is bad stakeholder management. We must understand what is involved in projects to diversify our project management approaches according to each one of them (Shenhar, 2007).

---

[5]CHAOS Knowledge Center. The Standish Group. Accessed on 20 July 2012, www.blog.standishgroup.pmresearch.

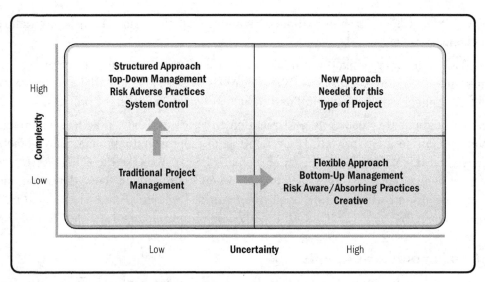

Figure 1-5: Project management approaches (Hartman, 2000).

Forget complaining that customers never know what they want. They do not dominate all the aspects of the problem nor its solution. If your client knew everything involved to execute a project that solves the problem, then the client probably wouldn't hire you. The client would do it himself! When buying, hiring, or contracting another company, the organization needs something that it doesn't have and that it cannot produce alone.

Stakeholders are (or should be) worried about their core business. And we have to manage all of them. We have to show or sell the benefits of our project's result to everybody and try to convince and persuade them to support us.

Author Dale Carnegie (2009) says that people are only interested in themselves and states that the best way to have someone do what you want is make him want to do it. Show the benefits, convince and persuade. This takes us back to the objective of this book: managing stakeholders as clients.

I state that every stakeholder is a client.

And, to support this statement, I give you a definition of client: someone that gives you something in exchange for another thing. As a project manager, you should know the "something" that you need from "someone." You know what you need (information, support, resources, and more), and you know who can give you that (stakeholders). But, will the stakeholders cooperate? Yes, as long as you give them "another thing,"; i.e., they have to want to do it, and they must want to help you. So, you need to discover what is important for your stakeholders and you have to connect their expectations to the project's goals.

Don't confuse this *client approach* with manipulation.[6]

You have to act as a seller, but as an honest seller. You receive a fair price for what you sell. Consequently, you'll get what you want from your stakeholders *if* you give them what they want. That's the deal: agree and exchange.

It's not easy to apply this client approach to stakeholders because they don't understand, most of the time, the results and the impacts of our project. You have to inform them, listen to their worries, influence their expectations, and persuade their decisions. Think of this like coaching your stakeholders. You should get to know them and find out what benefits your project can generate for them.

Imagine you have a billion-dollar project. You'll have to work hard to sell it. You simply can't finish it and succeed without selling its benefits to your stakeholders.

In fact, the complex sales approach is intrinsically related to the inspirational leadership. The inspirational leader should have the ability to inspire others by casting a vision for individuals and groups of stakeholders (Goleman, 2006) and the leader must connect their expectations to the project's goals.

---

[6]Dale Carnegie also reminds us that we must be genuinely interested in other people (our stakeholders?). That's partnership! Being manipulative or fake is not only morally wrong but also foolish because in the end, your allies will turn their backs on you. You can't deceive everybody forever.

Chapter 2

Who Are They?

If you know yourself but not the enemy, for every victory gained you will also suffer a defeat.

Sun Tzu

2.1 What Kinds of Stakeholders Can We Have?

Maybe you are a little confused about the objective of this book previously stated. We want to manage every stakeholder as a client. Even stakeholders against our project will be treated as clients.

And the client is always right, right? No. You are probably arguing that the *enemies* of your project cannot be seen (or treated) as your clients! They are against you! What would you exchange with them?

Well, fair enough. I have to agree a little bit. However, even these stakeholders are (or should be) clients of your project. The problem is that your project is threatening them, and they are offering resistance in exchange. If you try to see them as clients, you will want to know their needs, desires, and expectations about your project. By doing that, you could find a way to convince them or you can change your project to please them. If none of these *specific solutions* work, at least you know what they want, you will have to deal with them (stakeholder management). Anyway, you must know all your stakeholders to please them and to defend yourself and your project against them.

The first step in a project, after developing the project charter, is to identify stakeholders. This process can be a little tricky because of the complexity of your project; you could virtually affect the entire world. Using stakeholder's categories can help you.

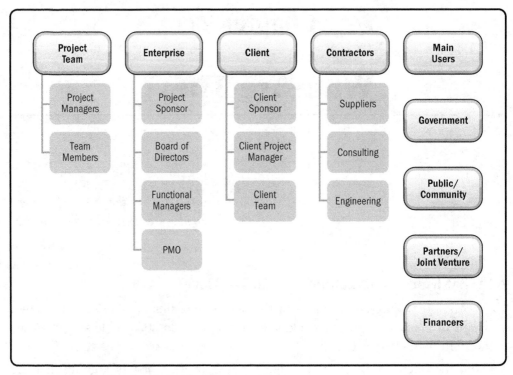

Figure 2-1: Example of stakeholder's categories.

Although categories are generic and broad, keep in mind that stakeholders must be identified individually. You can't assess and manage expectations of virtual entities.

Table 2-1: Example of stakeholder's register.

Stakeholder Name	Category	Friend or Foe	Objectives	Management Strategy
John D.	Functional Manager	Foe	Compete for resources	Show him the benefits of the new system
Mary A.	Workforce	Friend	Represent users and workforce	Ask her opinion Give her feedback
Anthony R.	Sponsor	Friend	Be promoted	Keep him always updated
Gill B.	Government	Friend	Protect taxpayers	Provide documents and reports about safety
Andy W.	Public	Foe	Protect environment	Establish a public relations plan
Anne T.	Contractor	Friend	Have profit	Discuss solutions with contractors Elaborate detailed SOW and contract
Charles A.	Team Member	Friend	Self-development Autonomy	Identify team member's needs Delegate wisely
Richard H.	Team Member	Foe	Work in another project	Give feedback Offer training

2.2 Project Manager

The project manager is probably the stakeholder that you know better, isn't he? Well, maybe not. We eagerly want to know more about the world, learn new knowledge, and obtain external knowledge. But do we take the right time to get to know ourselves?

Assess your own values and get to know yourself. You'll only be able to lead by example if you behave in a way that inspires example. Another aspect of self-knowledge is that you'll better deal with people if you know what motivates you. Develop soft skills and emotional intelligence to deal with other people.[7]

As a project manager, you will be seen as a leader, and you have to act like a leader. Your stakeholders expect this from you.

The project manager is the leader of the team. In large difficult projects, you might have thousands of people working in different teams, and you'll manage a core team that coordinates the other teams. Keep in mind that people are not simply human resources; they are individuals who get the job done. And every individual has his or her personal characteristics, skills, and expectations.

The project manager's role involves setting goals and direction, protecting the team, and influencing and persuading stakeholders.

The project manager must set boundaries, provide guidance, inspire, and coach the team to solve their own issues in favor of the project objectives. The project manager must also ensure these:

- The project's objectives are clearly stated.
- The project is effectively planned.
- The project's execution is monitored and controlled.

Clear objectives make possible drawing key success factors and prioritizing project's goals. In the end, the project's success will depend on the stakeholders' happiness or approval, which is directly linked to the objectives earlier stated.

One of the worst monsters in project management is ambiguity. Poor communications are the root cause of many project failures. So, considering communications, it's always better giving more information than necessary. And remember to be transparent and honest with your stakeholders.

2.3 Sponsor

The sponsor is not only who gives you money. Besides funding your project, sponsors have other very important roles in project management.

---

[7] There are good books about these topics, and I wouldn't like to be repetitive here. This book is about managing or dealing with stakeholders as clients; we are not going to talk about the project manager's self-improvement. I recommend that you take a look at *Emotional Intelligence for Project Managers*, Anthony Mersino (Amacom, 2007).

During the project life cycle, the sponsor acts as a focal point of escalation for the project manager and as high-level decision maker considering business and organizational context in which the project operates.

At first glance, it may appear that a project sponsor duplicates the efforts of the project manager. However, an experienced project sponsor can improve communication and coordination on issues beyond the project manager's responsibilities (Englund & Bucero, 2006). The sponsor's role is directly linked to senior management and includes these:

- Participating in project's selection and categorization;
- Participating in prioritization and resource allocation;
- Aligning project's objectives and business objectives;
- Monitoring and reporting on project progress to senior management; and
- Mentoring project managers.

It's easy to see that senior managers and top executives play an important role and have a big influence on projects' successes (Englund, Graham, & Dinsmore, 2003). The creation of project management offices (PMOs) is a step toward integration between strategic planning and project execution, promoting not only standardization and training for project managers and team members but also generating excellence in sponsorship to support projects.

The sponsor should add value to the project. In general, sponsors should have strong business and communications skills. He will act more like a visionary leader for the project, while the project manager will play management and technical roles most of the time.

Especially in intricate large projects, project managers need a lot of help from senior-level executives. And a sponsor is a senior manager who has a high level of authority and business experience. As stated before, the sponsor is a high-level decision maker for the project, which usually gives the project more agility and flexibility to adapt and absorb changes.

Considering the main topic of this book, sponsors are the ultimate project seller. They should sell the project to upper management before it starts and should protect the project during execution. However, finding good sponsors is difficult. Even organizations with high maturity in project management have problems in sponsorship (Englund & Bucero, 2006).

A good sponsor is the link between the project manager and senior managers and performs different functions during the project life cycle, promoting and protecting the project. The sponsor is involved with project selection and prioritization, well before the project starts.

During a project's initiation, the sponsor should be responsible for the project charter containing strategic linkages and the project's objectives. The sponsor should assign a project manager who can help write the project charter.

Project planning will be assigned to a project manager and that person's team, but the sponsor should participate and approve the project's plans. When the project is set up and running, the sponsor will monitor its progress and status and report to senior management.

The sponsor and project manager should have regular meetings to enforce trust and to keep information updated. The sponsor must ensure that the project's benefits are being delivered.

Project issues beyond the project manager's authority have to be discussed and decided by the sponsor. The sponsor must enforce the project manager's authority and legitimacy, giving credibility to the project.

2.4 Team

The project team will get the job done. They are going to carry out the execution. Team members are individuals, not replaceable resources. And their highest value is not in their technical competence but in their interactions and collaboration.

There must be a strong relationship, open communication, and confidence between the project manager and his or her team and between the team members as well.

It is very difficult to build a real team that can perform at its highest. More-over, it takes time. Figure 2-2 shows the four stages of team building according to Tuckman (1965).

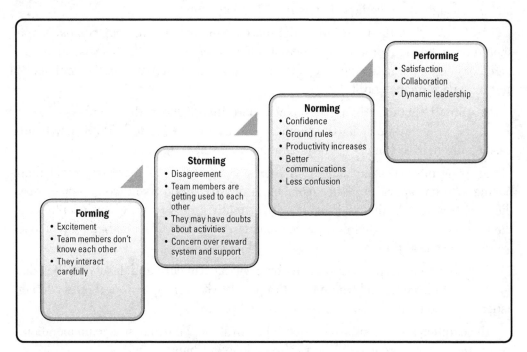

Figure 2-2: Team building stages adapted from Tuckman (1965).

In the beginning, at the forming stage, project managers communicate the project goals, set priorities, and direction. They should explain not only technical characteristics but also business aspects of the project to give a big picture to the team members. There will be a lot of excitement at the beginning of the project. People will introduce themselves to each other and get to know their workmates. The project manager acts like a leader who inspires.

At the storming stage, the project probably will be in execution. The execution team will be bigger than the management or planning team and some confusion might happen here. There might be disagreements about responsibilities, doubts about activities, and personal conflicts. The role of the project manager here is to guide, orient, and help solve conflicts. The project manager acts like a leader who enables other leaders.

To get to the norming stage, the project manager must help the team to set their own values and ground rules, so they can have a common agreement base. Confidence must be built by open communications, honest feedback, and transparency. The project manager acts like a leader-coach, setting boundaries and rules to separate the team from the outside. The team will be more productive as it acquires cohesion.

You'll probably be a lucky project manager if you can build a high-performance team. These teams, using Jurgen Appelo's (2011) words, must be grown. At this stage, team members will be satisfied, more like friends than only workmates. They will help each other, collaborate, and there will be dynamic leadership. The project manager's role here is to reinforce goals; the team members are supposed to be mature enough to define how they will get the job done.

As I said, it's difficult to build high-performance teams. In your company, you should try to keep them working together after the project is over. It's wise to assign them, or most of them, to other projects in a row, so they can maintain the confidence and high performance built.

A word of caution: when you replace more than 30% of the members of your team, you probably won't have a team anymore. You'll have to build a new team, passing through Tuckman's (1965) team building stages again.

Keeping internal stakeholders on your side is sometimes more important than having external approval. When your team doesn't support you, your project may die from treason. On the other hand, with a tightly united team, where people trust themselves and cooperate toward a common goal, you have a much better chance to overcome external threats.

Loyalty is something that you can't buy; you have to earn and deserve it. Besides good communications and true interest in people who work with you, there's another aspect you should care about: recognition and rewards.

Recognition and rewards are essential motivators. We will assess team members' needs and how to take care of their expectations in Chapter 7.

2.5 Clients and Users

There are many different definitions for clients and users. However, almost everyone agrees that they are different.

Clients and customers are usually associated with buying. They have the money, and they pay for what they want to buy. When managing a large involved project, you should be careful to find out who is your client.

We can have an internal client or an external client. When we have an internal client, it's probably easier to discover who that person is. The internal client is a senior manager or director who is responsible for funding or paying for the project. Most of the time, the internal client and the sponsor are the same person but that's not a strict rule.

You can have an internal client who is not the same person as the sponsor. In that case, you should pay attention not only to your sponsor but also to your client.

When a company hires another company to develop a project, we say that the buyer company is the client. We have an external client. Although the buyer company, as a whole, is the client, our job as project managers is to find out who is the person directly involved as a client inside the buyer company. We can't manage expectations of virtual entities. There's no way to assess what are the expectations of company XY, the buyer. You must identify a person, maybe a director or CEO, who is your real client inside the buyer company, to assess and manage that person's expectations. It might be a group of people, two or more vice presidents, for example. The idea is that you have to individually identify your clients, be they internal or external.

On the buyer's side, you can have a sponsor and one or more clients. There can be also a project manager from the buyer's and other points of contact. You should also map and communicate with these folks.

When we start talking about users, a new problem appears. We have direct users, which are easier to identify and map. However, we can also have indirect users, people who will probably work with the results of your product or service.

For example, suppose we are starting a project to implement an enterprise resource planning (ERP) system. Our direct users will be the workers who will use the ERP in some way periodically. However, we have other categories of users that would include IT support and management teams, suppliers, customers, and more. When you implement an ERP, you might also change some processes and procedures in your company, which will probably span your tree of user's categories.

Mapping all these direct and indirect users is a cornerstone to requirements identification and management. The client's satisfaction, most of the time, is strictly tied to the user's satisfaction. And this will result in project success.

2.6 Contractors and Suppliers

Commonly you'll have suppliers and contractors in large projects. The first assumption, as a project manager, should be that no contract will protect you from a bad contractor.

It doesn't matter what kind of clauses you create, the most useful advice is: choose your contractors and suppliers with care. Your contractors and suppliers will affect the scope and quality of your project. They may cause you damages not only with bigger costs and late schedules but also they may ruin your reputation with a failed project.

We think that partnership is an essential aspect that the project manager should be concerned about.

There are three main different types of organizations (Hull, 2011):

- Buyers: organizations that are acquisition oriented.
  They purchase and integrate systems to provide an operational capability. These organizations are mainly concerned with creating and managing stakeholders' requirements, which subsequently are used as the basis for acceptance of the delivered system.
- Sellers: organizations that provide systems, products and services solutions. These organizations respond to acquisition requests. They receive input requirements and provide solutions, which may involve developing system requirements and design before production. There are ranges of supplier levels from selling components to providing new systems solutions.
- Independent product developers: organizations that produce products and services to end-customers. They develop and sell products. These organizations collect stakeholder requirements from their marketplace; they are not oriented to individual business-to-business customers.

In large intricate projects, we may act like buyers, and our contractors will be sellers. From the buyer's side, the project manager should focus on creating good requirements that can be tested or measured when we receive deliverables from our seller. These requirements, obviously, must be aligned with project demand and goals.

We can also act like sellers, managing a big project to satisfy buyer's needs. In this case, the project manager should pay attention to collecting requirements and managing buyer's expectations. It's not uncommon that the buyer has a problem he wants solved but he doesn't know how the solution must be. It's the seller's role to clarify the problem so he can design and provide a solution.

Many companies act like independent product developers; they gather market information and create their products and goods. Innovation is an important competitive advantage and there may be challenging multifaceted projects being developed totally inside the organization. In this case, project managers have to focus their attention on internal stakeholders and their conflicting requirements and expectations.

2.7 Government

Government is virtually a stakeholder of every company and every project. After all, the government is responsible for ruling our countries and society, establishing laws, and creating ways to monitor if these laws are being respected. Large intricate projects must always observe applicable laws, standards, and everything that affects it. Lawyers and specialists in different areas might help the project manager to design and manage the project according to what is allowed.

We may need authorizations and approvals from government agencies for constructing, for developing a new drug, and so on. It's important that we identify and map individual stakeholders that we have to deal with. I mean, your stakeholder is not "the government," a virtual entity whose expectations you can't assess and manage. Your stakeholders should be identified as Table 2-2 outlines.

While a simplified example, the table illustrates the idea. Although we have the government as a stakeholder, we must find out what little pieces of government are directly related to our project. Then we must identify individuals and their expectations, so we can deal with them.

Large projects usually have big impact and side effects that might be addressed by law. It's wise to keep government inspectors involved. Your project can also be influenced by lawmakers and new legislation, so you have to watch their moves and pay attention to what risks could be created.

Although the government represents people and society in general, sometimes we have to consider groups of interest and communities that are more directly affected by our projects. In these cases, these stakeholders have to be included, involved, and managed. Their requirements and expectations should count and their interests must be mapped.

Depending on your project size, scope, and complexity, you might consider planning public relations and assigning responsibilities related to it.

Table 2-2: Governmental stakeholders.

Name	Agency	Role	Expectations	Management Strategy
Elliot Z.	FAA	Inspector	The aircraft project must satisfy all FAA requirements	Development strategy Systems Engineering
Kim O.	Air Traffic Control (ATC)	Manager	The aircraft must satisfy ATC requirements	Project planning
Eva S.	Airport Authority	President	Airport security	Tests design
Joan K.	State of XX	Governor	Taxpayers approval Workers' safety	Employment Safety
Gerald Y.	Public Bank of YY	Senior Manager	Return on investment	Solid business plan

2.8 Hidden Stakeholders

No matter how careful you are, it's not uncommon to have hidden stakeholders. Of course, we'll have less hidden stakeholders if we do a better identification job.

To help in stakeholder identification, it is useful to think about the following types of stakeholders (Clarkson, 1995; Frooman, 1999):

- Primary stakeholders – those ultimately affected, either positively or negatively by the project
- Secondary stakeholders – those that are indirectly affected by the project

Hidden stakeholders can be the most dangerous because they usually reveal themselves when projects are in advanced stages, when costs of change are higher. Another problem is that stakeholders are not islands. They are connected by lines of influence in a network of expectations where "commodities of power" (Checkland, 1990) can be exchanged. Moreover, stakeholders change their minds along the way; enemies can become supporters and vice-versa. As an example, Olander and Landin (2005) describe two case studies of construction projects that were delayed for about 10 years because of changing relationships and expectations of stakeholders.

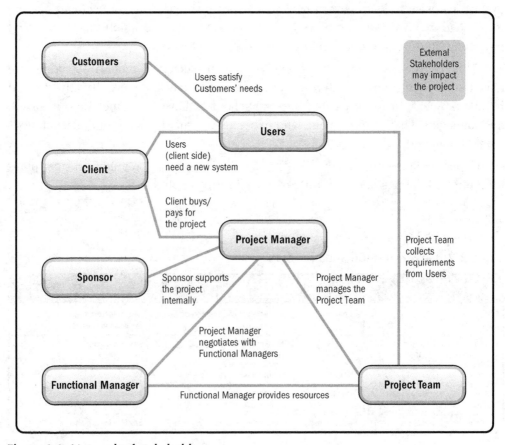

Figure 2-3: Network of stakeholders.

In this section, I'd like to reinforce and give you some advice on categories or types of stakeholders that you should care about. Remember that I told you a stakeholder breakdown structure is helpful for you not to forget some of them. You can also have a stakeholders checklist.

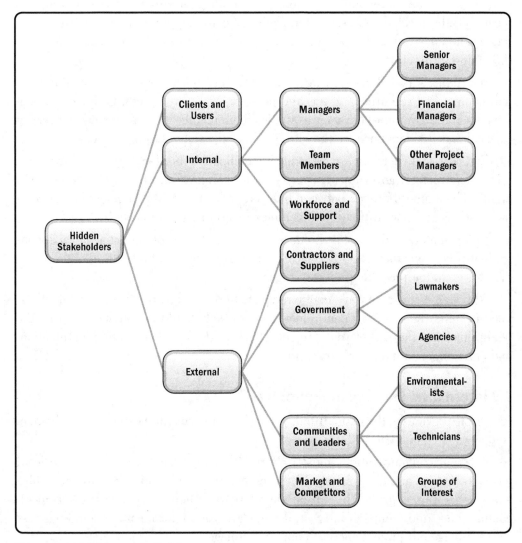

Figure 2-4: Hidden stakeholders.

Never forget to thoroughly identify individual clients and users that have power over the project. Usually, it's easier to identify clients because they pay for the project. They give us the resources.

Remember that we must identify them individually. Suppose company XTE hires you to develop a new aircraft. XTE is your client, but who are the decision makers inside that company? They are your individual clients, and your project must satisfy their needs. So, you have to map and manage them and their expectations.

Users are most of the time more difficult to identify. We might not only have plenty of end-users but also other users. For example, if your project is supposed to develop a new car model, you have groups of end users that will buy cars for their own. Besides the driver and his friends or family that will use the car, you also must consider mechanics, assemblers, sellers, spare suppliers, manufacture operators, even pedestrians, and police, just to name a few users. Projects can have many direct and indirect users.

Internally, stakeholders may worry about their status and comfort zone. Managers will compete for resources, power, and prestige. Workforce might be worried about job cuts and extra work-hours, for example. Team members are a special category of internal stakeholders because they are intrinsically related to the project.

External stakeholders are beyond our company's borders. We can have suppliers, contractors, government, society and communities, groups of interest, and others. The main difference between internal and external stakeholders is that communications are more difficult and complex externally than internally.

Unfortunately, hidden stakeholders have a bad habit of popping out at inconvenient times and they usually have negative expectations and attitudes that were overlooked in the previous project's stages.

Although I can't give you a magic recipe to find out who are all your stakeholders, keep in mind that this is a continuous process that should be carried out from the beginning until the end of your project. Don't overlook stakeholders' identification, and don't underestimate their importance.

2.9 Internal vs. External Stakeholders

As I wrote previously, the main difference between internal and external stakeholders is how we communicate with them.

External communications must be formal because they are subjected to legal terms, contracts, and agreements. Moreover, external communications might involve a large spectrum of groups like in public relations. When we deal with government, communities, and groups of interest, there is great room for misunderstandings that could damage our project and our company's image.

Jack Lemley, formerly chief executive of Transmanch-Link (TML), stated that managing the public image of major civil engineering projects is at least as important as managing their physical creation (Wideman, quoted in Cleland et al., 2004).

Poor public perception can damage a big project. Actually, a bad image can cause the project to stop by public pressure. Large involved projects, when dealing with external stakeholders like government, communities, and groups of interest have enormous risks to cope with. A good risk management approach includes stakeholders' management and public relations. It's much better to obtain support and buy-in in advance than counteract or react to overcome adverse public opinion.

Besides solid public relations management, the project manager must build a network of value, not a chain value, among contractors and suppliers. The project manager must be responsible for the project's quality. If a supplier or contractor delays or provides bad services or materials, your project's objectives will be affected.

The golden lesson for project managers is that the client is not the only real stakeholder to worry about. The project should add value for all the stakeholders, considering various dimensions like environmental, social, political, economic, etc. No matter if stakeholders are primary or secondary, internal or external, you have to pay special attention to key stakeholders, the ones that have significant influence upon or importance to the project.

Chapter 3

Why Worry About Them?

Big projects have a higher chance of failure than small projects,
primarily for sociological and communicative reasons.

DeMarco and Lister

3.1 Stakeholder Theory

The Stakeholder Theory was originally defined by Edward Freeman (1984). He identified groups of stakeholders and recommended methods by which companies' management could cope with the expectations and interests of those groups.

As new groups of pressure started to influence or impact companies, a concern was born that shareholders were not the only ones important to companies. That motivated Freeman (1984) to create the term stakeholder, encompassing all people and groups that could affect or be affected by a company.

Since then, the word "stakeholder" has assumed a prominent place in management theory and practice. In a broad sense, according to Bryson (2003), this term refers to persons, groups, or organizations that must somehow be taken into account by leaders, managers, and front-line staff.

Bryson (2003) enumerates some variants of stakeholder definitions:

- *"All parties who will be affected by or will affect [the organization's] strategy (Nutt & Backoff, 1992, p. 439)*
- *"Any person group or organization that can place a claim on the organization's attention, resources, or output, or is affected by that output" (Bryson, 1995, p. 27)*
- *"People or small groups with the power to respond to, negotiate with, and change the strategic future of the organization" (Eden & Ackermann, 1998, p. 117)*
- *"Those individuals or groups who depend on the organization to fulfill their own goals and on whom, in turn, the organization depends" (Johnson & Scholes, 2002, p. 206)*

Despite the similarities in the definitions of stakeholders, there is some controversy about the power of stakeholders. Some authors like Eden and Ackermann

(1998) defend that stakeholders are people or groups who have the power to directly affect the organization; absent that power, they are not stakeholders. In contrast, other authors (Bryson, 2004; Trentim & Lyra 2010; Mitchell, Agle, & Wood, 1997) urge consideration of a broader array of people, groups, or organizations as stakeholders, including the nominally powerless.

Bryson (2004) defends that including the powerless as stakeholders would seem to be more compatible with typical approaches to democracy and social justice, although there is no explicit ethical content in any of the definitions above. In my opinion, to include or not the powerless is a pragmatic decision, especially in project management.

The definition of stakeholder that we choose affects who and what counts (Mitchell, Agle, & Wood, 1997). By experience, I know that even "powerless" stakeholders can be very dangerous to projects. Remember also what I mentioned before about networks of stakeholders: stakeholders are not islands, they change and move while interacting in a network of interests where power can be exchanged or combined.

Donaldson and Preston (1995) quoted in Alexander (2005) proposes a model with three circles that represents, starting from the center, the Normative, Instrumental, and Descriptive aspects of stakeholder theory.

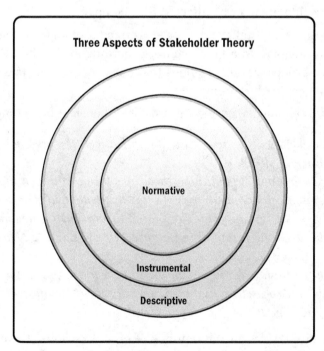

Figure 3-1: Three aspects of stakeholder theory (Alexander, 2005).

"The external shell of the theory is its descriptive aspect; the theory presents and explains relationships that are observed in the external world. The theory's descriptive accuracy is supported, at the second level, by its instrumental and predictive value; if certain practices are carried out, then certain results will be obtained. The central core of the theory is, however, normative" (Donaldson & Preston, 1995, p. 74, quoted in Alexander, 2005).

To make stakeholder theory more practical and in order to help its use in project management, I use an analogy to the model proposed by Donaldson and Preston:

1. Normative: who and what counts (stakeholder identification, which depends on project management governance)
2. Instrumental: how to assess stakeholders' interests and influence (stakeholder analysis, which depends on the project management methodology adopted)
3. Descriptive: strategies to engage stakeholders and manage their expectations (plan stakeholder management, which is usually a choice of the project manager and his team)

In summary, stakeholder theory states that organizations need stakeholder support to create and sustain winning coalitions to guarantee viability and sustainability. Projects, as temporary endeavors of organizations, also need stakeholder management; otherwise, they are in great danger of failing. The success of a project depends on the satisfaction of key stakeholders, who must be satisfied (Hartman, 2000).

My last advice in this section is that you consider stakeholders in the broadest sense possible in order not to turn a blind eye to stakeholders that could impact your project in the future. It is wiser to begin any stakeholder identification and analysis with a more inclusive definition.

3.2 Needs vs. Wants

People will be happy when you satisfy their needs. But you have to find what the real needs are (Hunter, 1998). It's kind of obvious that before you can find a solution you must conduct a thorough problem definition. Considering that project success is a matter of perception in the eyes of stakeholders, they must be involved all the time.

Needs will become requirements in different levels that will limit design options to provide a solution. The solution can be seen as a system designed or engineered to solve the problem proposed. This system will be developed based on specifications related to the original requirements, which in turn are tied to the real needs. This is called "virtuous cycle," where all requirements and specifications have traceability links to satisfy the real needs.

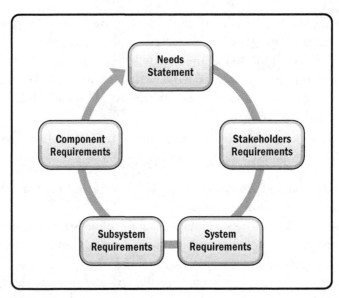

Figure 3-2: Virtuous cycle of traceability.

As we have mentioned throughout this book, we are facing challenging complex and large projects. If ever project management and systems development needed consistent methodologies, they certainly do so today. Fast-changing technology and scenarios as well as increasing competition are pushing us to comprehend how to create solutions that fit in the big picture of complex problems. It's kind of like shooting moving targets. And these situations lead to a common error: taking effects for causes.

We are getting addicted to using boilerplates, half-cooked and black box solutions, without understanding what the problem and its implications are. Most of the time, it's not that we can't see the solution; we are not seeing the problem.

Problem identification is the first step to success. This should be done during a project's selection and prioritization. However, the project manager is responsible for asking questions to make requirements clear and uncover potential forgotten needs.

From the project point of view, after formally initialized by a project charter, the project manager must identify the stakeholders and have them to map their expectations. Requirements elicitation will be the next step and should also be conducted very diligently.

Before we discuss requirements elicitation, it is important to mention surrogacy. A surrogate stakeholder is someone that plays the role of another stakeholder. For example, a team member can be a surrogate customer, in case you do not have direct access to the customer. This is usual when developing mass products like a cell phone. Marketing acts as a surrogate of potential customers to elicit requirements of the product.

The potential for misunderstandings arises as the gap between the surrogate and the real stakeholder is greater. Contractual interfaces can also bring more misunderstandings.

We will study stakeholder identification and analysis thoroughly in Chapters 6 and 7.

3.3 Requirements Elicitation

According to IEEE-STD-1220-1998, a requirement is a statement that identifies a product or process operational, functional, or design characteristic or constraint, which is unambiguous, testable, or measurable, and necessary for product or process acceptability (by consumers or internal quality assurance guidelines).

This broad definition points out some important aspects. It reminds us of the famous SMART rule of thumb: requirements must be specific, measurable, agreed to, realistic, and time-bounded. Above all, a requirement defines something necessary for product or process acceptability. But who will accept the product or process?

Stakeholders will vote on project success and they will accept a project's results. That's why requirements elicitation must be carried out diligently.

Collecting requirements is not only talking to stakeholders and writing down their "needs." It is a continuous progressive and iterative process. You can benefit from using different techniques, such as these:

- PDCA
  o Plan, Do, Check, Act
- IDEAL
  o Initiating, Diagnosing, Establishing, Acting, Leveraging
- DMAIC
  o Define, Measure, Analyze, Improve, Control
- SPIN (complex selling approach)
  o Situation, Problem, Implication, Need of Payoff

There are other approaches and all of them can be useful under different circumstances. Whatever kind of techniques you use, keep in mind that this process of requirements elicitation is a creative and cognitive process. You can even use multicriteria decision analysis tools and techniques like the Soft System Method (SSM).

Requirements are the basis for every project, defining what the stakeholders need. The challenge is to capture requirements, understanding stakeholders' needs, completely and unambiguously. Remember, requirements must be SMART: specific, measurable, agreed to and realistic. Every requirement should have objective criteria to assess its satisfaction.

To be well understood by everybody, it's common to express stakeholders needs in natural language to provide high-level requirements for the project. Specialists will work out to transform these needs into system and components requirements and specifications.

We all know that needs and requirements can change over time; our project is a living entity bounded by constraints that also can change. That's no problem. If you have a sound requirements and configuration plan, you'll do okay. In this way, requirements provide both the "navigation chart" and the means of steering towards the selected destination (Hull, 2011).

Now that you've understood the importance of good requirement elicitation, how do we do that in a real world? I've already emphasized the importance of communications. We could summarize three kinds of skills you must possess to succeed (Englund & Bucero, 2006):

- Gathering
  - o focuses on customers' and users' needs
  - o understanding businesses
  - o technical knowledge and experience
- Talking
  - o communications skills
  - o interviewing
  - o building relationship
- Follow-up
  - o planning
  - o prioritization
  - o traceability and change management

Information gathering focuses on the customer and on the users. Learn what the problem is, how the solution should be, and how it might be used to solve the problem. Business understanding, environment assessment, and behavioral observation are techniques that could be used. The project manager will also take advantage of prior knowledge and experiences.

Talking focuses on building a relationship, which means having the right information. Trust and commitment are key success factors during the project life cycle. The project managers have to be proactive in dealing with facts and anticipating needs.

Finally, follow-up focuses on management decisions that involve planning, organizing, and managing requirements and scope.

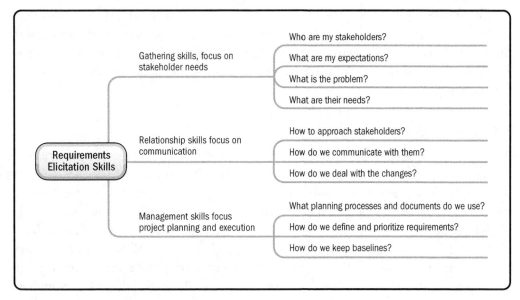

Figure 3-3: Requirements elicitation skills.

Keep in mind that requirements elicitation and system definition also face challenges related to political and commercial factors, interactions among multidisciplinary teams, conflicting viewpoints of stakeholders, and technical and technological issues.

It is usual to prioritize requirements. The acronym MoSCoW is well known for addressing this issue and coping with the challenges mentioned above:

- Must have – essential requirements
- Should have – important requirements
- Could have – nice to have requirements
- Won't have – establishes what is the scope and what is not the scope of the product or project

Clients and users are essential sources of requirements (Englund & Bucero, 2006). However, there are other very important stakeholders who should be involved in requirements elicitation. The complete life cycle of a product or system needs to be considered in order to collect requirements. Tradeoffs between maintenance costs and production costs, for example, have to be considered. Section 7.3 contains procedures to collect requirements.

As we are going to see in the next section, traditional engineering methods are failing to anticipate all requirements needed to secure a solution that satisfies the stakeholders' needs because of the increase in complexity of new systems. Systems engineering is a multidisciplinary and collaborative approach used to derive, evolve and verify a system solution, composed of products and the organization implementing the products' life cycle processes, balanced throughout the system's life cycle to satisfy stakeholders' needs and get public acceptance. The products and the organization composing the system solution are developed concurrently.

3.4 Systems Engineering

According to INCOSE (2004), Systems engineering is an interdisciplinary approach and means to enabling the realization of successful systems. It focuses on defining customer needs and required functionality early in the development cycle, documenting requirements, then proceeding with design synthesis and system validation while considering the complete problem: Operations, Performance, Test, Manufacturing, Cost and Schedule, Training and Support and Disposal. Systems engineering integrates all the disciplines and specialty groups into a team effort forming a structured development process that proceeds from concept to production to operation. Systems engineering considers both the business and the technical needs of all customers with the goal of providing a quality product that meets the stakeholders' needs.

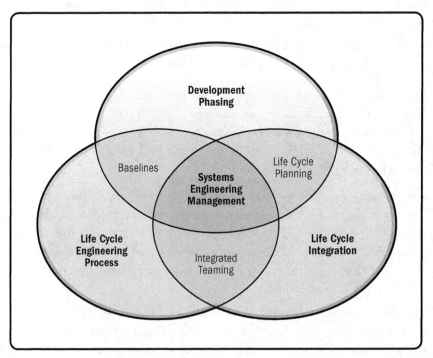

Figure 3-4: Three activities of systems engineering management (Defense Acquisition University, Systems Engineering Fundamentals, 2001, Fig. 1-1).

As an interdisciplinary and multidisciplinary field, Systems engineering focuses on how intricate engineering projects should be designed and managed throughout their life cycles. Systems engineering consists of two significant disciplines: the technical knowledge domain in which the systems engineer operates, and systems engineering management.

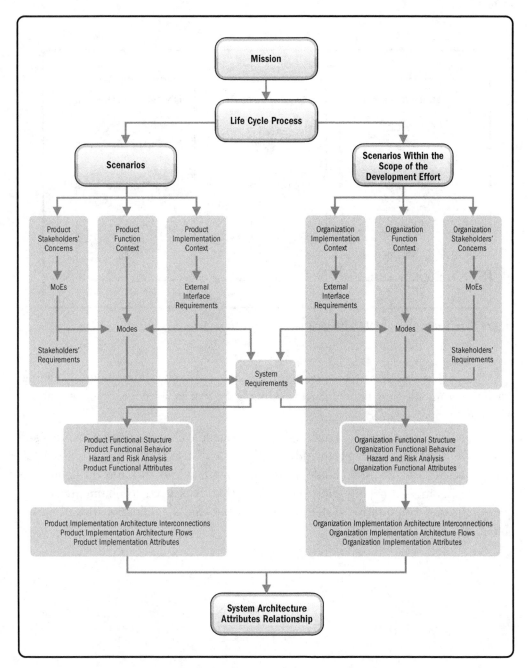

Figure 3-5: Systems engineering processes.

In one sense, Systems engineering fills the gap between project management and technical disciplines by providing a set of tools, techniques, and best practices for building complex systems and systems of systems. Some popular techniques of systems engineering are USL (Universal System Language), UML (Universal Modeling Language), QFD (Quality Function Deployment), and IDEF0 (Integration Definition).

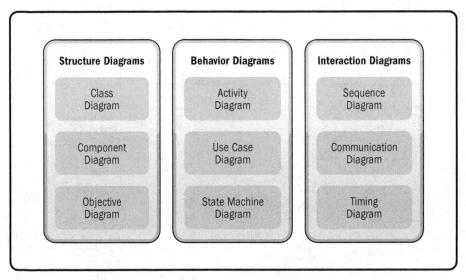

Figure 3-6: Examples of UML diagrams.

On the other hand, Systems engineering enables systemic thinking and modeling. An interesting starting point for developing a system is its concept of operations (CONOPS).

A concept of operations is a document describing the characteristics of a proposed system from the viewpoint of an individual who will use that system (1362–1998 IEEE). You can gather stakeholders' perspectives or views to build different concepts of operations and integrate them. A CONOPS is used to communicate the quantitative and qualitative system characteristics and specifications to all stakeholders to satisfy their needs.

Table of Contents

Title/Paragraph		Page Number
Preface		
Executive Summary		
Revision Summary (if applicable)		
Section 1:	Introduction	
Section 2:	Operations and Support Descriptions	
2.1	Missions (primary/Secondary)	
2.2	Users and Other Stakeholders	
2.3	Policies, Assumptions and Constraints	
2.4	Operational Description	
2.5	Mission Support Description	
2.6	Potential Impacts	
Section 3:	Scenarios	
3.1	Mission Operations Scenario(s)	
3.2	Mission Support Scenario(s)	
Section 4:	Functional Capabilities	
4.1	Mission Operations	
4.2	Mission Support	
4.3	Functional Capabilities Matrix	
Section 5:	CONOPS Development Team	
Section 6:	Appendices	
6.1	Analysis Reports	
6.2	Table of Changes	
6.3	Glossary of Terms	
6.4	Acronym Listing	
6.5	References	
List of Tables		
List of Figures		

Figure 3-7: Concept of Operations Table of Contents (Concept of Operations Template, Defense Acquisition University, https://acc.dau.mil/CommunityBrowser.aspx?id=245888).

The CONOPS and the Statement of Needs are the basic documents to develop a system. They provide, preferably in natural language, the statement of goals and objectives of the system. As project managers, we can see the importance of these documents. We can make an analogy saying that the project charter must contain a business case and the statement of needs. In the beginning of the planning phases, the project manager and his or her team will focus on gathering information and collecting requirements, based on the Project Charter, to build a more detailed

Statement of Needs and to create a concept of operations document to provide information to subsequent planning processes and stages.

Requirements will provide the basis for planning the development of a system and accepting it on completion. They are essential when sensible and informed tradeoffs have to be made, and they are also vital when, as inevitably happens, changes are called for during the development process (Hull, 2011). Requirements therefore form the basis for these:

- Project planning,
- Risk management,
- Acceptance testing,
- Tradeoffs, and
- Change control.

Figure 3-8 shows the hierarchy of requirements. We can also see that there are different goals for every level, associating system development and acceptance.

We start from stakeholders' requirements, which by the way were obtained from stakeholders' needs (Needs Statement). Usually, the Needs Statement is written in natural language, avoiding technical jargon when possible. Then stakeholder requirements, the highest level of requirements of a system, are developed.

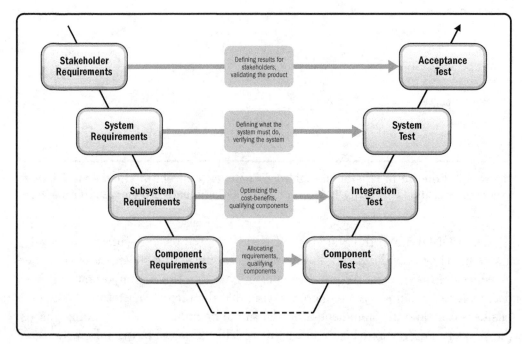

Figure 3-8: Requirements engineering in layers (Hull, 2001, p. 11).

When talking about requirements, we are in the problem domain. The problem domain includes those stages of development associated with the highest levels of system description—Statement of Need, usage modeling, and stakeholder requirements. The importance of defining the problem is somewhat obvious and requires adequate attention because subsequent layers in the solution domain will be supported by definitions in the problem domain.

The next step is defining system requirements, which is in the solution domain. The solution domain involves system requirements, system architecture and lower level requirements, such as subsystems requirements and components requirements.

You might already imagine that stakeholder management is essential in all levels and stages of system development. However, in the beginning, stakeholder management plays a more important role. When trying to define requirements, we have to find out what the needs are and we have to deal with competing demands and expectations from various groups of stakeholders.

Table 3.1: Problem domain versus solution domain.

Stakeholder Requirements	System Requirements	Architectural Design
Problem domain focused on stakeholder's view	Solution domain created by analyst's view	Solution domain created by designer's view
State what stakeholders want to achieve through use of the system, what stakeholders want to be able to do using the system. We are not worried about implementation, design or particular solutions. Always try to create requirements that are implementation free.	State abstractly what the system will do to meet stakeholder requirements. Still avoiding reference to particular design or solution.	State how specific design will meet the system requirements

3.5 Life Cycle and Scope Definition

Systems engineering's concepts give a broader view of scope definition and show how project management can benefit from using systemic thinking and modeling. Moreover, considering we are writing a book on how to manage stakeholders in complex large projects, we are probably going to deal with complex systems and products. Systems engineering will provide us with product-oriented processes, which are not covered in the *PMBOK® Guide*.

The *PMBOK® Guide* is about project management processes that ensure the effective flow of the project throughout its existence (Project Management Institute, 2008). These processes encompass tools and techniques involved in applying the skills and capabilities described in the Knowledge Areas (Project Integration Management, Project Scope Management, Project Time Management, Project Cost Management, Project Quality Management, Project Communications Management, Project Human Resources Management, Project Risk Management, and Project Procurement Management). The *PMBOK® Guide* contains good practices in project management.

However, a project is not only made of project management processes. Actually, the majority of a project is related to product-oriented processes; after all, we want to build something. This unique result will need product-oriented processes to be specified and created. Product-oriented processes are typically defined by the project life cycle and vary by application area.

Besides, the *PMBOK® Guide* states that the scope of the project cannot be defined without some basic understanding of how to create the specified product. Systems engineering comes to help us here: product-oriented processes. We will also need more specific processes from other disciplines and sciences such as engineering.

As the *PMBOK® Guide*, PRINCE2™ describes project management processes that coordinate how technical knowledge should be applied through product-oriented processes during the project life cycle. The defined roles of PRINCE2™ state an important distinction between the project manager and technical managers, or team managers.

Considering that in order to achieve control over anything, there must be a plan, management processes are carried out by the project manager. On the other hand, to build something, product-oriented processes are also usually needed, which implies technical knowledge of team members and team managers.

There are three basic types of project life cycles. We can have totally predictive life cycles, called waterfall, where it's possible to define its scope before execution. And we can have totally adaptive life cycles, sometimes called agile, which are driven by success factors that state what should be done next. In the middle, we have incremental and iterative life cycles.

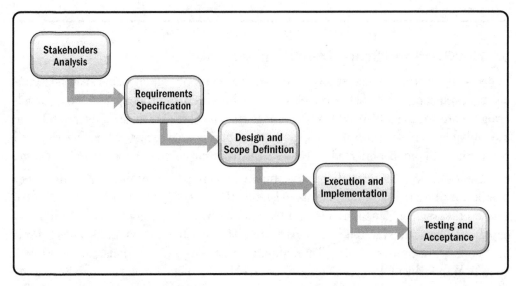

Figure 3-9: Predictive life cycle.

Predictive life cycles are used in well-known and established industries, such as construction, where one may be able to plan everything about the product and the project in advance.

These projects proceed through a series of sequential phases, as we can see in Figure 3-7. Each phase focuses on specific project activities using inputs from preceding phases and providing outputs to subsequent phases in a sequential fashion until the project is completed: the project team will focus on defining the overall detailed scope for the product and project and then develop a complete plan to deliver the product and finally proceed through phases to execute the plan within that scope.

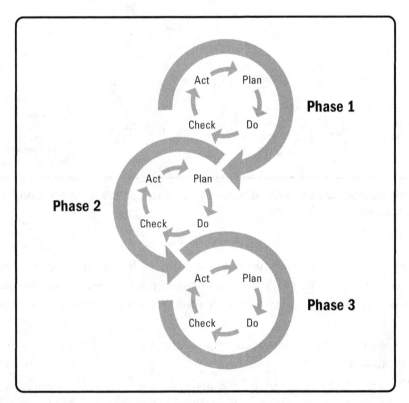

Figure 3-10: Incremental and iterative life cycle.

It's not unusual that projects have overlapping phases. Considering timing and other pressures faced by projects nowadays, it's becoming common to use incremental, progressive, and iterative life cycles. These life cycles are intended to deliver projects faster.

A high-level project scope is generally determined early in the project life cycle, but time and cost estimates are routinely modified as the project team's understanding of the product increases. Iterations provide detailed specifications while developing the product through a series of repeated cycles. Every phase or stage has its own plan – do – check – act cycle, respecting the high-level project scope defined in the project initiation.

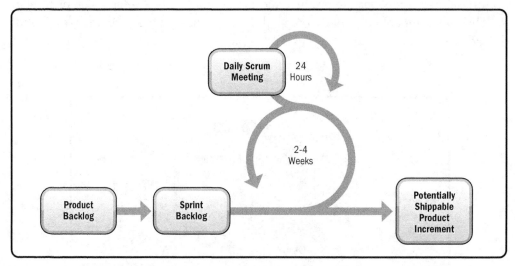

Figure 3-11: Adaptive life cycle (Mountain Goat Software, 2005, Licensed Under Creative Commons Attribution 2.5).

To cope with complex products and to deal with timing pressures, adaptive life cycles were created. Agile methodologies are focused on delivering value while discovering stakeholder needs in projects where scope is not completely defined.

Adaptive life cycles are intended to facilitate change and require a high degree of ongoing stakeholder involvement.

In PRINCE2™, according to the characteristics of a project, the project manager chooses, with the help of senior suppliers and maybe other stakeholders, a life cycle that best fits the project's purposes.

Managing by Stages, a core principle of PRINCE2™, structures the project's life cycle on a stage-by-stage basis. As agile approaches and iterative life cycles, PRINCE2™ enforce that planning can only be done to a level of detail that is manageable and foreseeable (OGC, 2009).

An analog to Scrum, which uses a prioritized backlog and sprint plans, PRINCE2™ has two types of plans: detailed team plans for the short term and an outline project plan for the long term. That overcomes the planning horizon issue and provides better management and control to projects.

3.6 Change Management

Change is inevitable during the life of a project. A systematic approach to the identification, assessment and control of issues that may result in change is a key success factor in project management (OGC, 2009).

The project manager is ultimately responsible for the project management plan and its success. With input from stakeholders, he plans the sequence of activities, works out how many resources will be required, provides and refines other project management plans needed.

It is impossible for the project manager to do the entire job. If one man can build the result himself, maybe a project manager is not needed. Project managers have to delegate and monitor project work. Ideally, projects should go according to plan, but frequently that's not the case.

Project plans will change. That's the "only certainty." Of course, this is not an excuse for mismanagement or bad monitoring and controlling in projects. It is the project manager's responsibility to monitor how the work in progress deviates from the plan and take action.

Remember the Plan-Do-Check-Act? There is no way to monitor what was not planned, there is no way to control what is not monitored, and there is no use trying to control without taking action. Whether it is by taking corrective or preventive actions or implementing measures to improve performance, the aim of project managers is to keep the project on track.

To help the endeavor of monitoring and controlling projects, change management should be based on a clear and formal process, so every stakeholder can understand it and its importance for the project's success. It's not meant to be a cumbersome or bureaucratic procedure that makes changes difficult.

Of course, to implement good change management, it's essential to start with clearly defined and agreed requirements, and this takes us back to requirements elicitation and scope definition advice mentioned in previous topics. But, change management must also answer these questions:

- What is under change control and what is excluded?
- How are changes requested?
- Who has the authority to approve or reject changes?
- How are decisions on approval or rejection documented and disseminated?
- How are changes implemented and their implementation recorded?

  The *PMBOK® Guide* has a special process to manage changes: perform integrated change control.

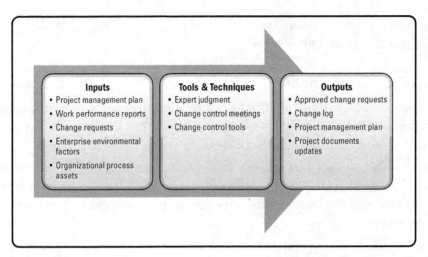

Figure 3-12: Perform integrated change control (Adapted from the *PMBOK® Guide—*Fourth Edition, PMI, 2008).

As we can see, this process tries to answer the questions proposed previously. While developing the project management plan, we must include a subsidiary plan: change management plan. This plan defines these:

- What is under change control and what is not;
- Change requests templates;
- Change management analysis and approval process; and
- Change log and status report.

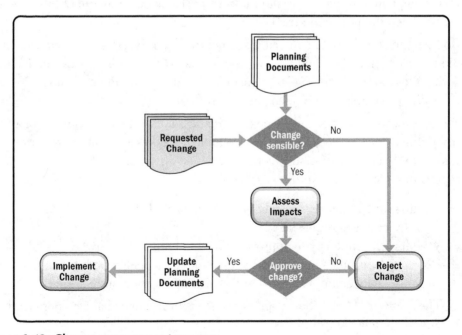

Figure 3-13: Change management process.

The simplified change management process shown in Figure 3-13 is a great starting point. You must define a formal change management process in your project, specifying what must be done in each stage.

First, every change request must be standardized. Once received, the project manager has to assess if change is sensible, according to the project management plan and other project documents.

It's usual to have a change control board to help in assessing impacts and deliberating on alternatives to the change request proposed. A change control board is a group of people responsible for approving requested changes and assisting in the assessment and prioritization of changes. This group is generally composed of senior specialists in different technical and business areas involved in the project.

It's important that the authority and responsibility for approving change requests must be clearly stated. If approved, all planning documents must be updated before implementing change.

Although change is inevitable, we can't fall into the trap of ever-changing scope. This will result in scope creep and a failed project in the end. Consequently, as project managers, you must exercise saying no.

Invariably, users and clients will ask for plenty of changes during project execution. This is something like the Red Queen's Race[8]: users and clients frequently want more features than they need, just in case...

A golden rule is to never accept a change request instantaneously. A formal change management process is critical. You'll have time to discover if the client really needs that change while you are assessing its impacts on your project. Then you'll better manage stakeholders' expectations (client) and make informed decisions. Otherwise, change requests can become a snowball.

Configuration management is the technical and administrative activity concerned with the creation and maintenance of up to date configuration of products throughout the life of the project. Specifically in large intricate projects, there is a huge effort in systems engineering and in keeping requirements traceability to assure that the product will satisfy stakeholders' needs. Look at Figure 3-14, and you'll have a big picture of what is involved.

---

[8] The Red Queen's race is an incident that appears in Lewis Carroll's Through the Looking-Glass and involves the Red Queen, a representation of a Queen in chess, and Alice constantly running but remaining in the same spot. [Source: Wikipedia]

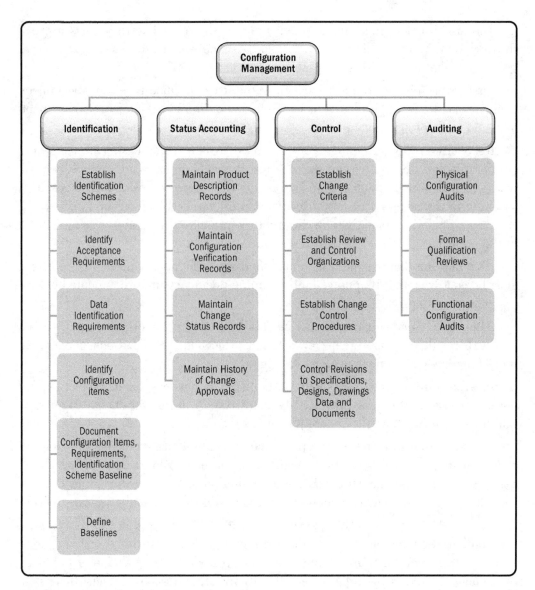

Figure 3-14: Configuration management.

Change is a theme in PRINCE2™, which describes how project management assesses and acts upon issues that have a potential impact on any of the baseline aspects of the project (OGC, 2009). A PRINCE2™ change management procedure is represented in Figure 3-15.

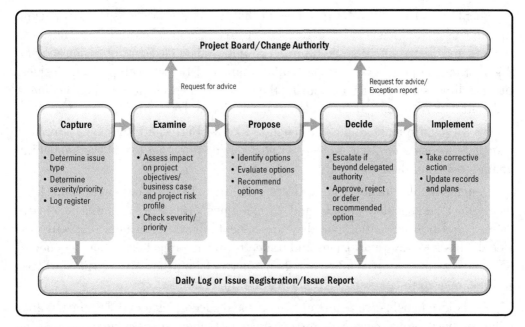

Figure 3-15: Issue and change control procedure (OGC, 2009, p. 95, Fig 9.1).

3.7 Success in Project Management

There are four ways to close out a project: extinction, addition, integration, and starvation (Meredith & Mantel, 2000; Stewart & Sheremeta, 2000). Extinction means the project is terminated because it achieved its goals successfully. Addition and integration are different ways of a project being absorbed by operations of the organization. Starving is when resources are dried out and the project simply dies without reaching its planned end.

No matter how a project is terminated, even by extinction, success cannot be evaluated only internally. Success is a measure of benefits generated not only by a project but also by its outcomes. However, we all know that achieving success can vary with the type of project. Actually, success in projects is hard to define.

The triple constraint (scope – time – cost) is certainly one important aspect. On the other hand, as Peter Drucker (2008) says, there is nothing so useless as doing efficiently that which should not be done at all. So, we have to think of concepts like business value added, return on investment and project benefits management.

Classic measures of project management success like on time, on budget, and meeting specifications are not enough anymore. The real measure of success is related to stakeholders' satisfaction.

Remember Francis Hartman's definition of project success: happy stakeholders (Hartman, 2000). When I say stakeholders, I mean not only clients and users but also every other stakeholder who votes on project success leading to benefits management.

Shenhar and Dvir (2007) recommend that we assess project success by using five dimensions: efficiency, impact on the customer, impact on the team, business success and preparation for the future. The importance of each dimension may be different among projects due to particular characteristics of each project. Besides, success dimensions may change during the project's life cycle, as new information is gathered and as the environment changes (Shenhar & Dvir, 2007).

It's difficult to manage project benefits, I know. But, what's the point of project managers focusing on their projects without paying attention to what is happening around them and their company?

Benefits management begins with the definition of key success indicators (KSI) that reflect stakeholders' needs and expectations. These KSIs must be clearly defined and prioritized because they are benefits-driven indicators that will provide the basis for future decisions and tradeoffs during project execution. Of course, KSIs must be measurable and reasonable. You can follow the SMART rule for KSIs: specific, measurable, agreed to, realistic, and time bounded.

To achieve benefits, you must identify critical success factors (CSF), factors that influence positively or negatively project success. Critical success factors are essentially enterprise environmental factors and organizational process assets. Identifying CSFs is an important part of planning and will be part of monitoring and controlling along project duration.

Finally, business value is a concept that is unique to each organization. Business value is defined as the entire value of the business; the total sum of all tangible and intangible elements (Hubbard, 2010). Concluding, project success depends highly on value propositions, how they are delivered to and perceived by key stakeholders.

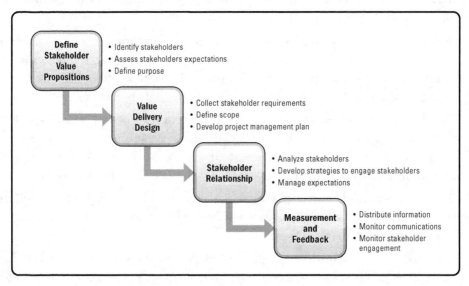

Figure 3-16: Satisfying stakeholder value propositions.

Business value is created by effective management of operations, strategic planning, and effective use of projects, programs, and portfolios. Particularly, portfolio management must be aligned with corporate strategy, so projects can provide benefits and business value added. In a way, project's benefits start with portfolio selection and prioritization. On the other hand, the project manager's role is to assure benefits achievement.

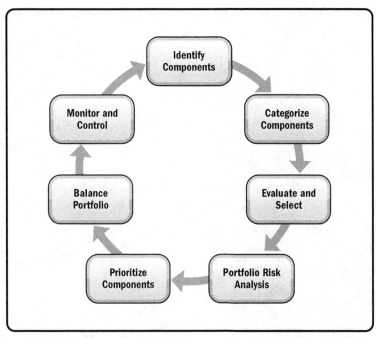

Figure 3-17: Portfolio management processes (Adapted from *The Practice Standard for Portfolio Management*, PMI, 2008).

Continuous Business Justification is a principle of PRINCE2™ to maintain the project's purpose on the spotlight along the way. In PRINCE2™, there should be a justifiable reason to start a project and the justification should remain valid throughout the life of the project, which is assessed periodically in stage reviews (OGC, 2009). The justification is documented and approved in a business case.

PRINCE2™'s business case changes and evolves during the project life cycle. The justification may change, but it is essential that it remains consistent. That is, the project is still worth doing and there should be a justifiable purpose for that. If, for whatever reason, the project can no longer be justified, the project should be stopped in order not to waste the organization's effort and resources.

Chapter 4

The Four Ships

A project is successful if all the stakeholders are happy.

Francis T. Hartman

4.1 Sponsorship

Sponsorship is crucial to successful projects. When managing large intricate projects, the project manager must understand the importance of senior management support and make whatever possible to pave the way for good sponsorship.

We've talked about the role of a sponsor and shown sponsors as leaders protecting the project and acting as the ultimate sellers for the project. If project sponsors spend time with their project manager, project team, and customer, they will know more about the projects that are so important for their livelihood. They will be more effective and potentially generate more business (Englund & Bucero, 2006). On the other hand, it's part of the project manager's role to connect with the sponsor and to help build this relationship.

Multifaceted projects need sponsors who are more leaders than managers are. The project manager is the manager, the lieutenant responsible for managing tactical-operations activities at the project level, including planning and executing. The sponsor is more like a general who sees the big picture, an experienced leader able to establish directions for the future, communicate through vision, and help in creating aligned high-performance teams. The sponsor, sometimes, will mentor to help the project manager.

Both the sponsor and the project manager must cooperate and collaborate to add value to the project. Their responsibilities are complementary and play important roles at different decision levels inside and outside the project environment. The sponsors provide authority to the project managers, so they can lead their teams and accomplish their missions.

Along the way, making decisions will be necessary. The sponsor will make business decisions that are supported by project decisions made by the project manager. The sponsor promotes and defends the project in front of all other project stakeholders, while the project manager is focused primarily on the project itself.

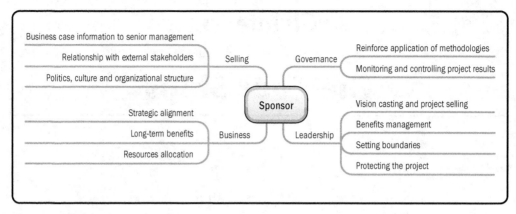

Figure 4-1: The sponsor's role.

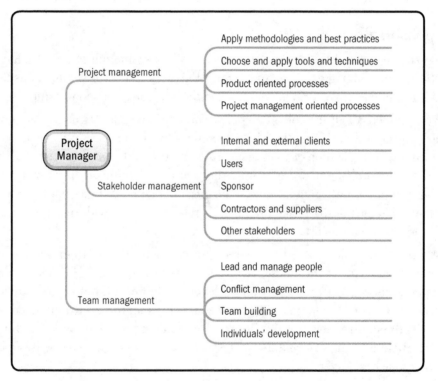

Figure 4-2: The project manager's role.

Few sponsors or stakeholders will support product or systems development without a clear business case and a convincing risk management strategy. Therefore, the project manager is responsible for proper planning to get buy-in and support from sponsors and other stakeholders.

Remember that the larger the project, and the longer its schedule, the higher the chance of failure. Some sources even claim that the odds of successful completion of a project disappear almost completely with large-scale projects (Yourdon, 2004, quoted in Appelo, 2011).

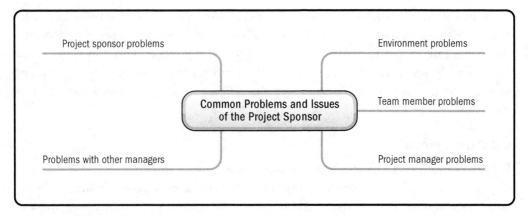

Figure 4-3: Common sponsorship problems.

PRINCE2™ address sponsorship by involving three dimensions of interests in every project: business, suppliers and users.

While the principle of *Defined Roles and Responsibilities* states that a project has defined and agreed roles and responsibilities within an organization structure, the theme *Organization*, in PRINCE2™, establishes project management levels with specific roles and responsibilities.

Figure 4-4: The four levels of management within the project management structure (OGC, 2009, p.33, Fig 5.2).

The Project Board is composed of an executive (business interests), senior(s) supplier(s) and senior(s) user(s). The executive plays the role of sponsor. However, the entire Project Board provides sponsorship to the project. Also, the principle of *Continued Business Justification* implies the involvement of an executive, resulting in every project having a sponsor. However, the same Project Board can sponsor more than one project.

4.2 Partnership

Why partnership? It's kind of obvious that project managers must focus on sponsorship and leadership to succeed in their projects. However, a project manager is not only going to deal with sponsors and team members. The project manager, most of the time, will have to build trust among different contractors, suppliers, and even real partners in joint ventures. Moreover, project managers will have to deal with clients, customers, and users.

When we think of partnership, competition and negotiation comes to mind. Actually, from a systemic point of view, multiple agents often compete for the same resources. In nature, agents might try to have each other for lunch.

Charles Darwin, when discussing the survival of the species, mentioned fitness. Fitness is the ability to exist and to prosper. Like success in project management, fitness is relative (imagine a lion in the ocean). In other words, fitness could be the ability to build systemic sustainable relationships. Consequently, understanding the environment is crucial to succeed.

If we think of project results, the fitness of a product is determined not by its conformance to requirements, but by its benefits and the ability to satisfy the stakeholders. Let's define partnership to understand how it is related to fitness and success in projects.

> Partnership: cooperation, association, collaboration, coalition, alliance, union, relationship, connection, consortium, syndicate.

We have some synonyms of partnership in this list. From this list, you can imagine how important this dimension is to your project. Besides, stakeholders will probably create partnerships among them. As a project manager, if you ignore that, your circle of influence may be limited and you can face more difficulties in establishing and maintaining supportive coalitions.

In every kind of partnership, it's important that all partners share bonuses and onuses in a way that is agreed. As a project manager, especially in large intricate projects, keep in mind that your project relationships will last for a long time. First, a project may take several years to be accomplished, and second, because probably you'll meet some of the same partners in future projects.

People need to know each other well to do business together. The more you know about the project and its environment, the easier it will be to build relationships with stakeholders. Building trust is essential because lack of trust can seriously undermine cooperation. It will be much easier to solve problems when you reinforce partnership.

We will see negotiation, communications, and interpersonal skills later on. We will also talk about legal agreements and contracts to support partnership, especially when dealing with external stakeholders like clients and suppliers.

4.3 Leadership

Leadership is the golden dimension. In Stephen Covey's (2004) words, you manage inventory, you manage cash. But you lead people.

Leadership means casting a vision in a way that involves people and makes the vision happen. Wow, that's project management!

Good leaders are also managers. You can't lead without assessing, guiding, and giving feedback to your followers. Some people create a wall between leader and manager, which is not good. Actually, you can be a manager without being a leader, but you can't be a leader without management skills.

The manager is seen as the chief, boss, organizer, and controller. The manager rules because he or she is invested in authority. On the other hand, the leader is a guide, coach, and mentor. While management is related to supervision and command-and-control, leadership is about influence and relationship. You have to master both leadership and management to be a successful project manager. But what does it take to become a leader?

As in other professions, project managers are more effective when they are passionate in their approach to projects and people. They need to reinforce best practices, often more than once, and explain why those methods make the most sense. To ensure that project activities are done the right way, project managers need to be persistent. And in taking the necessary time to talk with people and solve problems requires that they be patient (Englund & Bucero, 2006).

Passion, persistence, and patience are qualities of good leaders. We are going to talk about leadership styles and how to develop them later on this book. For now, experts James Kouzes and Barry Posner (1993) identified six practices that they called the six "disciplines of credibility."

1. Explore yourself. To be credible, clarify your own values and beliefs so that you can act accordingly.
2. Be sensitive with team members. Listen to and protect them, understand their values and desires. Cultivate respect.
3. Confirm shared values. Manage diversity and create common ground rules and values for agreement on which everyone can stand.
4. Develop capacity. It's important to develop people. You have to map their knowledge, experience, and capacity, so you can provide them with training, challenges and coaching.

5. Serve a purpose. Leadership is a service.
6. Sustain hope. Credible leaders keep hope alive even in troubling times of transition. Always have a positive attitude.

Cleland (1986) also believed that attitudes play an important role in the management of a project. He says that a positive attitude allied to proactive management of stakeholders enhances the probability of a successful project. Moreover, positive and proactive attitude can reduce the chances of the project team being surprised and unprepared for adverse situations (Cleland, 1986).

4.4 Citizenship

We are all parts of groups and communities. And we also are citizens of the world. Recently, sustainability issues have arisen in many projects. Now we have to worry not only about direct stakeholders but also about indirect stakeholders such as the general public.

In fact, every person is motivated by internal values. And these values today include social responsibility, environmental protection and more. We can summarize citizenship as conscience.

As a project manager, be aware. The first rule is be ethical. The second rule is be responsible. The third rule is be trustworthy by always following the first and second rules.

A sense of citizenship brings us to hard decisions involving tradeoffs between alternatives, especially between present actions and future consequences. It is very important that the project manager builds a strong purpose and provides clear priorities.

Citizenship, as leadership, can be assessed. In fact, stakeholders will be watching your project.

Because of the increasingly interconnected nature of the world, projects are not restricted to the inner world of the organization that executes it anymore (Bryson, 2004). Instead, many stakeholders are involved in or affected by the project.

Bryson (2004) goes on and says that:

> "we are moving into an era when networks of stakeholders are becoming at least as important, if not more important, than markets and hierarchies (Powell, 1990, quoted in Bryson, 2004) even if those networks are often operating in the shadow of hierarchy (Hanf & Scharpf, 1978), or in the shadow of markets (Milward, 2003)."

The PRINCE2™ relationship between outputs, outcomes, benefits, and disbenefits is very illustrative.

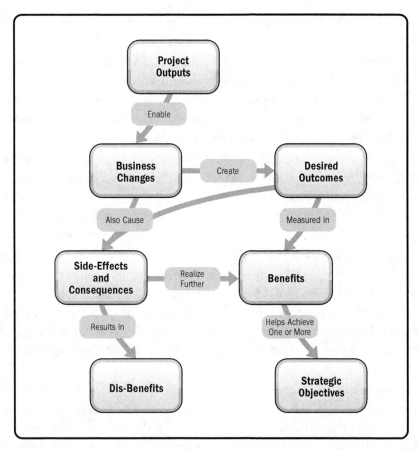

Figure 4-5: Relationship between outputs, outcomes, benefits (OGC, 2009, p. 22, Fig. 4.1).

A project has to be analyzed from different perspectives of stakeholders to understand its impacts in a "chain of benefits and dis-benefits."

When it comes to articulating and achieving the common good, people often need to be convinced that there is something that can be done about a problem before they will support (Freeman, 1984). As a matter of fact, the creation of private value at the expense of public value is not only unethical but also destroys business value in the long run.

I decided to add the *citizenship* dimension in project management because I believe in it. Once you lose legitimacy and credibility, it is very hard to get them back.

4.5 Fitness for Purpose

The objective for describing these four "ships" is to settle the basis for management practices. These core values will help you when you are in trouble and show you the right way. Although we have great-established methodologies and standards, like the *PMBOK® Guide*, none of them may cover all types of projects that we face nowadays.

So, my contribution with these general principles is to help project managers make better decisions.

Sponsorship constitutes the basis for a project. Without help and support, no project can endure. Moreover, sponsorship means that the project has a bigger chance of adding value to and being aligned with the corporate strategy. When we choose good projects by the right selection methods, we have a much better chance of success. We must execute the right projects right.

The second principle is partnership. Especially in large intricate projects, the project manager will deal with plenty of stakeholders, individuals, and groups. Trying to arrange conflicting requirements, expectations, and necessities of stakeholders is not easy. The ability to make alliances and partnerships, communications, and negotiation skills will be determinants for the project to succeed.

Leadership is kind of a fashion today. It's expected that everybody has leadership skills. Is that right? Leadership is misunderstood by most people. Project managers don't have to be like Abraham Lincoln or Alexander the Great. In management, leadership means enabling other people to develop their potential while nurturing and fostering a good environment for teams to grow. We don't need heroes and superstars. We need dream teams! People that work at their best together in a coordinated fashion.

Finally, citizenship is a stairway to success. I chose this word to encompass honesty, transparence, and values. We've been seeing a lot of frauds and lies for a long time. Some people may still be out of jail making millions at the expense of others. But this is not the way we do business or manage projects. If you are strong enough to stand for your values, you are the real project manager and a citizen of the world.

These four "ships," I hope, will guide you when in doubt.

As project managers, we will be responsible for setting standards. And it's never bad to raise the bar when we're talking about principles and values.

The next chapters will bring us less philosophy and more tools. You'll learn ways to identify stakeholders, assess their expectations, create strategies to engage and manage stakeholders, and build solid communications. You'll also learn how to get buy-in and sell your project.

Chapter 5

Stakeholders as Clients

Right or wrong, the customer is always right.

Marshall Field

5.1 Complexity

Definitions of complexity are often tied to systems.

We can think of a project as a system with many subsystems and components. Team members, suppliers, resources, and functional managers are examples of components. Actually, even the definition of a system and its boundaries is arbitrary. Depending on your choice, you can use different levels of abstraction.

By defining a system, we establish levels of subsystems, environment and super-system. When a system has many parts in an intricate arrangement, we say it is a complex meaning and we can't understand all the links and relationships between components and subsystems. The overall behavior of a system depends on its components and it is not predictable. Therefore, it is complex.

We have to distinguish complicated from complex. Complicated is difficult to understand, typically related to the structure. For example, solving an equation is complicated, but there is an established method to do so, and we can understand it. On the other hand, complexity is related to behavior and our ability to predict future behaviors. The stock market, for example, is complex. We are not able to model its behavior or predict its movements, especially in extreme events like economic crisis.

And what does complexity bring to us? When we don't understand something, we tend to go away from it. We want certainty. In the *Paradox of Choice*, Barry Schwartz (2003) gives us some interesting insights:

- When we have many alternatives and we don't understand every aspect, we are not able to differentiate them.
- When confronted with hard decisions, we tend not to decide.
- When we are faced with a lot of functionalities, we tend to commoditize products in our minds.

We are dealing with large intricate projects. They probably have many requirements and many details. Also, these kinds of projects have many stakeholders, interfaces, and influences, which makes them complex.

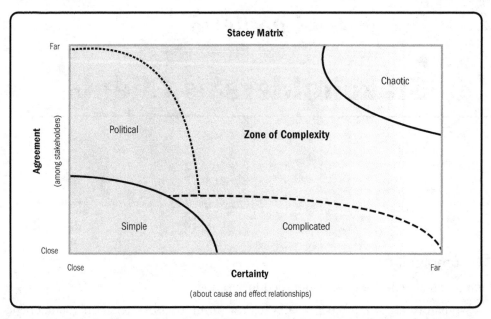

Figure 5-1: Complexity as a function of agreement and certainty (Stacey, 2011, 2012).

Figure 5-1 shows us that in the zone of complexity, problems and structure are difficult to understand, leading to a lack of certainty about solutions. To make matters worse, there are many stakeholders involved and a low degree of agreement both about the problem and its requirements and about possible best solutions and alternatives. And that's not all the bad news. The environment is changing for your project, your company, and everything else as you try to tackle the problem and get stakeholders agreement.

One way to lower complexity, from the project manager's point of view, is to teach and persuade stakeholders. The project manager must involve stakeholders in decisions and explain project details for them. Because if the project manager doesn't do that, he or she will face two huge problems. The first problem is change management due to bad requirements and poor understanding of stakeholders' problems. Managing stakeholders' expectations is extremely important. The second problem is what I call The Red Queen's Race.[9] It's the kind of scope creep caused by poor stakeholders' management. You need more than involving stakeholders, you must understand, influence, teach, and persuade them.

Noriaki Kano (1984) developed a theory on product development and customer satisfaction. The Kano Model classifies customer preferences into five categories:

- Attractive — provide satisfaction when achieved fully, but do not cause dissatisfaction when not fulfilled (attributes not normally expected)

---

[9]The term is taken from Lewis Carroll's book, where the Red Queen said to Alice: "It takes all the running you can do, to keep in the same place."

- One-Dimensional — result in satisfaction when fulfilled and dissatisfaction when not fulfilled
- Must-Be — are taken for granted when fulfilled but result in dissatisfaction when not fulfilled
- Indifferent — refer to aspects that are neither good nor bad, and they do not result in either customer satisfaction or customer dissatisfaction
- Reverse — refer to a high degree of achievement resulting in dissatisfaction and to the fact that not all customers are alike

The Kano model is used in product development. These categories of preferences guide the product's attributes to provide competitive advantage. Kano's model focuses on differentiating product features, while still satisfying known customer needs.

In project management, we can apply Kano's categories to help in stakeholder assessment and in managing stakeholder expectations.

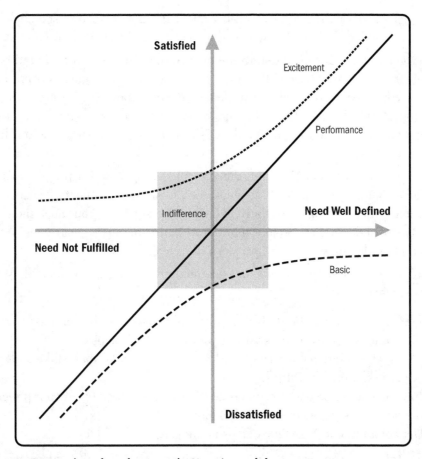

Figure 5-2: Categories of preferences in Kano's model.

To conclude, no wonder the CHAOS reports illustrates poor project results. Complexity is hard to tame. Despite that, proactivity is the breakfast of champions, paraphrasing Mersino (2007). If you don't manage complexity, your project will be "managed by chaos."

5.2 Our Approach to Stakeholder Management

Barry Schwartz (2003) also showed that when people don't understand the features of a product or system, they can't compare. So, they reduce their expectations to a common ground: price. On the other hand, it is common that customers ask for features they will never use and they always want more to feel updated.

We should be proactive, which means we engage and involve stakeholders, while also keeping control of the project by influencing, persuading and directing stakeholders in a learning process through the project. The alternative is letting stakeholders "manage" the project with the risk of an outcome detrimental to the project's objectives (Cleland, 1986), even hurting stakeholders' interests themselves.

All along the way, we've been talking about the importance of stakeholders for project success. It's obvious that we must involve them, but how do we do that?

The project manager must determine expectations and benefits desired by each stakeholder. This is the "price" that has to be paid for the needed deliverance and compliance from each stakeholder (Mikkelsen & Grundbog, 2007, quoted in Jepsen & Eskerod, 2008). "Price" has to be understood in a broad sense, not only as direct monetary payment. Price is any kind of reward tangible or intangible exchanged with stakeholders.

We can conclude that the role of a project manager and a project sponsor is intimately related to sales. And stakeholders are similar to clients, consciously or unconsciously demanding rewards in exchange for support. You must show stakeholders the benefits of your project in order to build supportive coalitions. And you have to do that during your entire project's life cycle.

Here we have a simple script for stakeholders' management, according to the complex sales approach:

1. Identify and understand: Know your stakeholders well. Gather insight into their values and expectations. Put yourself in their shoes.
2. Focus and relationship: Define what you want from your stakeholders and build a relationship with them.
3. Influence and persuade: Emphasize the value and benefits of your project and the need for support from stakeholders.
4. Get commitment: Show next steps and engage stakeholders.

In partnership, you must build win-win agreements. If stakeholders are forced to agree on something, they will not feel comfortable, and your project will run into difficulties in the future. Teaching, influencing, and persuading help mitigate this risk. Allow stakeholders to question and even bargain before accepting the responsibility.

After that, keep in touch! Good rapport is a valuable commodity that contributes greatly to project success (Englund & Bucero, 2006). But you have to feed and maintain the relationship. The project manager has to measure stakeholders' satisfaction and support along the project; this is part of the stakeholders' management plan.

According to Rackham (1988), clients don't buy features or advantages, they buy benefits. A benefit is how something meets explicit needs from stakeholders. We believe that all project stakeholders can be managed as clients, using a complex sales approach. In other words, customers don't want a product itself, they want to solve some problems themselves, or satisfy an existing need.

Rackham (1988) points out four stages in successful complex sales:

- Situation: general information about the stakeholder and his environment;
- Problem: worries and expectations of a stakeholder;
- Implication: what will happen if the problem is not solved, consequences for the stakeholder; and
- Need of payoff: how can I fix it and what benefits will this bring to stakeholders.

Rackham also said that the two most important stages are implication and need of payoff because the client, or stakeholder, must perceive benefits to support your project. It's not enough to provide superficial information and presentations to stakeholders; they will not be engaged or involved and might not be willing to help you. You must understand their needs and cast a vision where your project fits their expectations.

We will also use another interesting complex sales approach created by Jeff Thull (2007). In summary, Thull says, in addition to what Rackham (1988) did, is:

- Prospect the right client: In project management, find out who are the decision makers and key stakeholders.
- Problem diagnosis: statement of needs and requirements elicitation; get agreement.
- Develop the solution: define project scope; involve key stakeholders, teach and persuade them; partnership with contractors and suppliers; lead the team.
- Deliver what was promised: manage project execution; manage stakeholders' expectations.

Well, this topic could be like *selling for dummies*, but actually it is selling to dummies. . . can you handle that? We want to sell our project to dummies (stakeholders). Well they are not dummies about everything, but they are dummies about what it concerns to your project, most of the time.

In Chapter 8, we will get back to complex sales based on Rackham (1988) and Thull (2007), and we will create a step-by-step approach adapted for project management. PRINCE2™'s principles and themes will also help us in this endeavor.

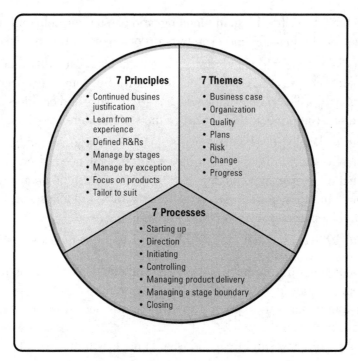

Figure 5-3: Summary of PRINCE2™'s principles, themes, and processes.

5.3 Lasting Relationships

You don't do a project, and then go away. A large multifaceted project lasts for months or years. In the meantime, you create a relationship with your stakeholders. You might even have to provide training, transition, and warranty time after the project is done. Besides, if you are dealing with clients, you will probably want to do business with them again. . .

When it concerns the project team, you will really have a lasting relationship. Team members are stakeholders. And they are extremely important because they get the job done! Anthony Mersino (2007) says that team members' selection is usually overseen by project managers, which causes problems during execution. He also said that he dedicates time to review and select team members, sometimes with the help of senior team members. Why? Because you will rely on team members to achieve project objectives.

And team members' selection is more than resume reviews; you have to assess not only knowledge and experience backgrounds but also emotional intelligence and team work. Of course, you will not do that with a thousand team members; however, you must dedicate time to select key team members that will be responsible for subprojects, so that they can build their own team in a project organizational structuring process.

It's interesting to note that research shows that teams perform much better when they are long-lived (Larman & Vodde, 2009). I believe success depends on good managers and leaders fostering team growth and providing guidance. However, most of this best performance comes from building communication paths and stating rules, which takes time to happen and show results.

It also takes time for them to learn, as a team, how to best make work division, handle problems, and solve issues and conflicts.

I've been paving the way for a stakeholders-oriented approach in project management. Sometimes it sounds like common sense; sometimes it sounds like utopia.

I hope that you are with me. Stakeholder management is extremely important. However, it is difficult to make it work. There is a lot of theory, but few practical guides on how to apply existing tools and techniques. Bryson (2004) says that there is relatively little literature on exactly how to systematically identify and analyze stakeholders. I believe it's very helpful to open project managers' minds using complex sales approaches allied to stakeholder theory in order to give life to tools and techniques described in the *PMBOK® Guide*, PRINCE2™, and other references.

Chapter 6

Identifying Stakeholders and Their Needs

I had no idea that such individuals exist outside of stories.

Sherlock Holmes

6.1 Stakeholder Engagement

As the opening quote of this chapter says, stakeholders' identification is part science (methodology, tools, and techniques) and part art. We'll give you science here. The art you will master with time and practice, developing social and emotional intelligence.

Stakeholder management in projects is the continuing development of relationships with stakeholders for the purpose of achieving a successful project (Jepsen & Eskerod, 2008).

In the *PMBOK® Guide—Fourth Edition*, we had stakeholder management inside the Project Communications Management Knowledge Area. There were two processes dedicated to stakeholders: identify stakeholders and manage stakeholders' expectations. These are other communications processes: distribute information and report performance.

In PRINCE2™, stakeholders are emphasized throughout as to their importance in managing projects. Particularly, the principle of *Defined Roles and Responsibilities* and the theme *Organization* (OGC, 2009) are more directly related to stakeholder management. We are going to explore in deep the *PMBOK® Guide* (Section 6.2) and PRINCE2™ (Section 6.3).

In broad sense, stakeholder engagement is the process of involving groups and individuals who may be affected by the decisions we make on projects or they can influence the implementation and execution of a project. This is a key success factor for projects.

Project managers must engage their stakeholders in dialogue to find out what their expectations are and what issues matter most to improve decision making and get buy-in.

An underlying principle of stakeholder engagement is that stakeholders have the chance to influence the decision-making process of a project. It's more than just stakeholder management and communication processes, which don't imply involvement and participation.

Engagement creates a sense of ownership and partnership, which leads to easier buy-in. Stakeholders must be committed to the project in order to support it.

These are some common failures in stakeholder engagement:

- Engaging with a stakeholder too late;
- Engaging the wrong stakeholders to participate; and
- Treating the participation of stakeholders as unimportant.

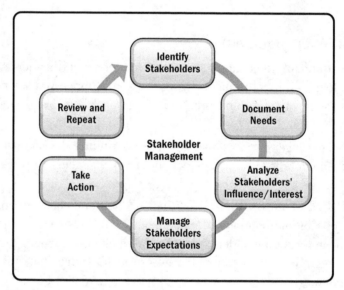

Figure 6-1: Stakeholder management cycle.

Project managers find several challenges in stakeholder management. Jepsen and Eskerod (2008) say usual guidelines lack clarity regarding how to identify stakeholders and determine their importance, and how to reveal or unveil stakeholders' expectations. Further, project managers may not have the skills or the resources required to carry out the tasks involved in managing stakeholders properly.

Frequently, stakeholder identification and stakeholder analysis are based on superficial rather than deep knowledge (Jepsen & Eskerod, 2008). Therefore, stakeholder management is inefficient and inefficacious, which creates some feeling of uselessness in trying to apply stakeholder management.

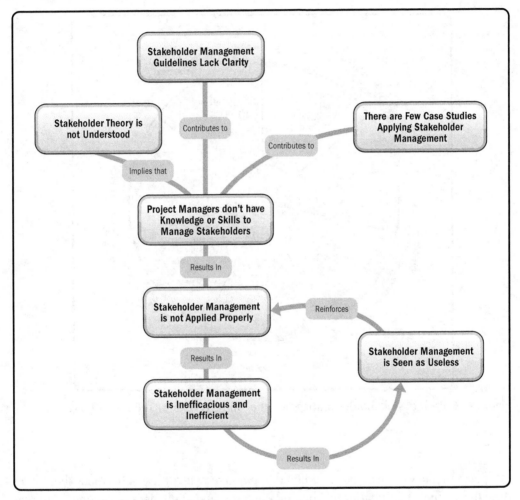

Figure 6-2: Challenges in stakeholder management.

There is a vicious cycle where stakeholder management uselessness is a result of its inefficacy and reinforces bad stakeholder management, which results in inefficacy. Despite that, stakeholder management has received considerable interest since Freeman introduced the concept in his book "*Strategic Management: A Stakeholder Approach*" (Freeman, 1984).

Project management literature also shows increasing interest in stakeholder management. However, there is a lot of study and research in describing and modeling stakeholder–manager relationships, while there is little research in using tools and techniques to manage stakeholders in practice.

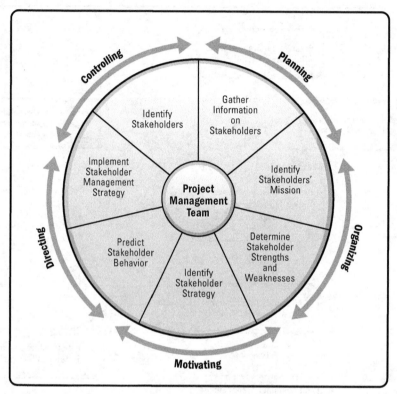

Figure 6-3: Project stakeholder management process (Cleland, 1986, p. 39, Fig. 1).

So, how do we carry out stakeholder management? First, attention should be directed to the identification of the stakeholders and their necessary contributions to the project. The next step would be to apply tools and techniques to stakeholder analysis. Then we would develop strategies and plan how to manage expectations along the way. And finally we would implement the stakeholder management plan, monitor and eventually take corrective actions.

We will see in detail how to manage stakeholders in the next sections.

6.2 What Does the *PMBOK® Guide* Say?

The *PMBOK® Guide*—Fourth Edition says that managing a project typically includes:

- Identifying requirements;
- Addressing the various needs, concerns, and expectations of the stakeholders as the project is planned and carried out;
- Setting and maintaining active communication with stakeholders; and
- Balancing the competing project constraints.

A stakeholder is an individual, group, or organization who may affect, be affected by, or perceive itself to be affected positively or negatively by a decision, activity, or outcome of a project (Project Management Institute, 2008).

Stakeholders can be actively involved in the project, such as client, sponsor, and project team members, or they can be passively affected by the project, such as the community.

In the case of stakeholders with positive expectations from the project, they must be engaged to support it. However, there can be stakeholders negatively affected by the project. Overlooking negative stakeholder interests results in higher risks. The project manager has to find ways to leverage positive expectations and lower negative impacts.

To deal with stakeholders in a proactive way, there are four main processes to focus on:

- Identify Stakeholders — The process of identifying all relevant people or organizations impacted by the project, analyzing and documenting relevant information regarding their interests, involvement, interdependencies, and potential impact on project success.
- Plan Stakeholder Management — The process of developing appropriate management strategies to effectively engage stakeholders in project decisions and execution based on the analysis of their needs, interests, and potential impact.
- Manage Stakeholder Engagement — The process of communicating and working with stakeholders to meet their needs/expectations, address issues as they occur, and foster appropriate stakeholder engagement in project decisions and activities.
- Control Stakeholder Engagement — The process of controlling overall project stakeholder relationships and adjusting strategies and plans for engaging stakeholders.

6.3 PRINCE2™

PRINCE2™, PRojects IN Controlled Environments, is a process-based methodology of project management. The United Kingdom Government uses it extensively, and PRINCE2™ is also widely recognized and used internationally.

PRINCE2™ is organized around *principles, themes,* and *processes. Principles* guide and inform how to apply the project management method. Similar to Knowledge Areas, *Themes* describe aspects of project management that must be addressed continually, and *Processes* address the chronological flow of the project (OGC, 2009).

Principles are universal, self-validating and empowering to provide a framework of good practice for project management. There are seven principles:

- Continued business justification – every project should have documented and approved reasons that justify its initiation and they need to be continuously reassessed and reviewed to ensure justification remains valid throughout the project life cycle.
- Learn from experience – teams start by looking for lessons learned, historical data and complementary knowledge about what will be the new project; knowledge management is a competitive advantage.
- Defined roles and responsibilities – clear and agreed roles and responsibilities engage and involve the right stakeholders to work for the project.
- Manage by stages – breaking down the project into smaller pieces helps in managing it because it is easier to control and plan in a shorter horizon, while still having a master plan to orient the project's objectives.
- Manage by exception – defining levels of authority and providing defined tolerances allow better delegation.
- Focus on products – in the end, what we want is the result of a project. A product-oriented approach focuses on quality and considers activities as a means to achieve product requirements.
- Tailor to suit the project environment – projects are different and their particularities have to be considered when choosing what processes, tools and techniques will be used as necessary.

Themes answer project management questions along the way in areas that are essential to managing a PRINCE2™ project. There are also seven themes:

- Business Case (why are we doing this project?)
- Organization (who is involved?)
- Quality (what are we going to deliver?)
- Plans (how will we execute the project?)
- Risk (what if? – uncertainties)
- Change (what's the impact of changing?)
- Progress (how is the project going? should we carry on?)

Processes orient the step by step of managing a PRINCE2™ project. There are seven processes:

- Starting up a project – authorize the initiation of a project to solve a problem or to seize an opportunity.
- Initiating a project – once the project is authorized, it is time to describe in detail what are the objectives, requirements and other information to document in a business case.
- Directing a project – this process encompasses the entire project and is carried on by the project board. The board reviews the business case and analyzes reports submitted by the project manager regarding progress and other issues.
- Controlling a stage – while the project board is in charge of directing a project, the project manager is responsible for controlling stages, which is day-by-day managing of a project: ensuring that the project management plan is being executed properly.
- Managing product delivery – while the project manager focuses on management processes, team members work to get the product done. Product delivery means product-oriented processes.
- Managing stage boundaries – at the end of every stage, the project manager reviews and updates documents according to the achievements of this stage. The detailed plan for the next stage is written.
- Closing a project – only the project board can officially close a project. The board closes a project based on the information provided by the project manager when formal acceptance of project's products has been given.

Processes "managing stage boundaries," "controlling a stage" and "managing product delivery" can be repeat in several delivery stages, considering the principle of "managing by stages."

Although we are not going further, PRINCE2's™ principles and themes provide important insights to stakeholder management.

I mentioned before some principles and themes, and we are going to use them as necessary in the next sections to help elucidate and guide stakeholder management.

6.4 Tools and Techniques

Is the government a stakeholder? It will depend on your stakeholder identification and on your project characteristics.

Well, we can also imagine that the government is usually a stakeholder of every project, directly or indirectly. If you say that the government is your stakeholder, how can you assess its expectations? How can you create a plan to manage the government's expectations?

We will review some tools and techniques to address these concerns.

Stakeholders' Identification

The identification of stakeholders must go beyond the internal stakeholders. External stakeholders provide a challenge to manage not only because they may not be as supportive as internal stakeholders but also because they are not subject to the legal authority of the project manager or the executing organization.

Further, care must be taken to identify all of the potential stakeholders, even those whose interest may seem initially irrelevant (Cleland, 1986).

Once a list of the stakeholders has been developed, it is time to gather information to make it more complete. The resulting stakeholder registry and documents are parts of the project management plan and should be reviewed periodically to determine if the stakeholders' perceptions or views of the project have changed.

Usually, we start by writing a list of stakeholders and then we add columns to the table (Table 6-1) to provide detailed information.

Name and contact information are always important. You may also include how to communicate with each stakeholder and what will be your strategy to engage or influence him or her.

Table 6-1: Stakeholders' registry.

Name	Contact Information	Agenda for the Project	Importance	Management Strategy

The complexity of the stakeholders' registry will depend on their influence and impact on the project, as well as the project complexity itself. Approaches that are more sophisticated may go beyond tables; you could use software to facilitate information storage and retrieval. Software can also help to communicate with stakeholders; something like a customer relationship management (CRM), while you communicate with stakeholders you also get and store more information to better manage their expectations.

Table 6-2: Stakeholders' registry.

Name	Contact Information	Priority/ Importance	Agenda for the Project	Values and Expectations	Areas of Interest	Role on Project	Communication Preferences	Strategy to Engage and Manage

Depending on the project, you may decide how much information to include in the stakeholders' registry. It's important to keep in mind that stakeholder identification will be the basis for stakeholder management and engagement.

According to the *PMBOK® Guide*, there are three steps involved in stakeholder analysis: identifying stakeholders, identifying potential impact, and assessing how stakeholders are likely to react to given situations (Mulcahy, 2009).

- Identifying Stakeholders: general information, contact information and project knowledge;
- Assessing Potential Impact: power/interest grid, power/influence grid, influence/impact grid, salience model; and
- Classifying Stakeholders: influence, expectations, potential negative impacts.

In the end, you can have a complete picture of your project stakeholders.

Table 6-3: Stakeholders' registry.

Name	Information	Priority	Friend or Foe	Agenda for the Project	Values and Expectations	Areas of Interest	Role on Project	Communication Preferences	Strategy to Engage and Manage
Mario H.	Phone Email	High	Friend	Support System Implementation	Transparency Reliability Wants Objective and True Reports	Product Quality and Performance	Sponsor	Weekly Meeting	Keep Informed Keep Involved

But where can we find information to fill these tables shown before? How can we discover who are the stakeholders of our project? One solution is to conduct brainstorms in which names of all the stakeholders are identified.

To properly build a stakeholder map, you will first need to identify who can give you information on key stakeholders. You can also get information about stakeholders using other sources like the media, press releases, company's information and so on.

You can ask known stakeholders of the project to point out other stakeholders. It might also be helpful to use generic stakeholder lists with categories of stakeholders, something like a checklist of stakeholders or a stakeholder breakdown structure.

It is extremely important to have in mind that you can learn just as much about the stakeholders by interacting with them as you can from the other sources mentioned above. One of the most efficient ways to learn about your stakeholders is by asking them pointed questions that involve different aspects of the project. However, this is not always possible and you may have to use surrogates, role-playing and other techniques to try to uncover stakeholders and their expectations.

Stakeholders' Assessment

Stakeholders have to be characterized as regards contributions needed from them, the expectations they have concerning rewards for delivering the contributions, and their power in relation to the project (Cleland, 1986). Information gathering involves answering the following questions:

- What information do we need to know about each stakeholder?
- Where and how can we find the information needed?
- Who will have responsibility for gathering, analyzing and interpreting the information?
- How can the information be protected from "leakage" or misuse?
- Who has responsibility for carrying on stakeholder management strategies?

The main objective of stakeholder analysis is to identify key stakeholders. Therefore, the final characterization parameter for stakeholders is the power that the stakeholders have with regard to influencing the project (Jepsen & Eskerod, 2008).

The vast majority of stakeholder analysis models use some variation of the power/interest grid.

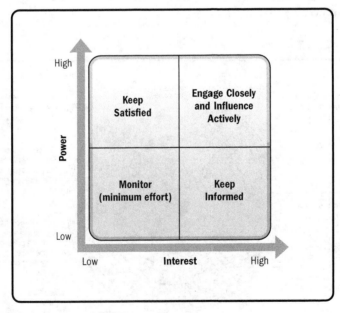

Figure 6-4: Power/interest model.

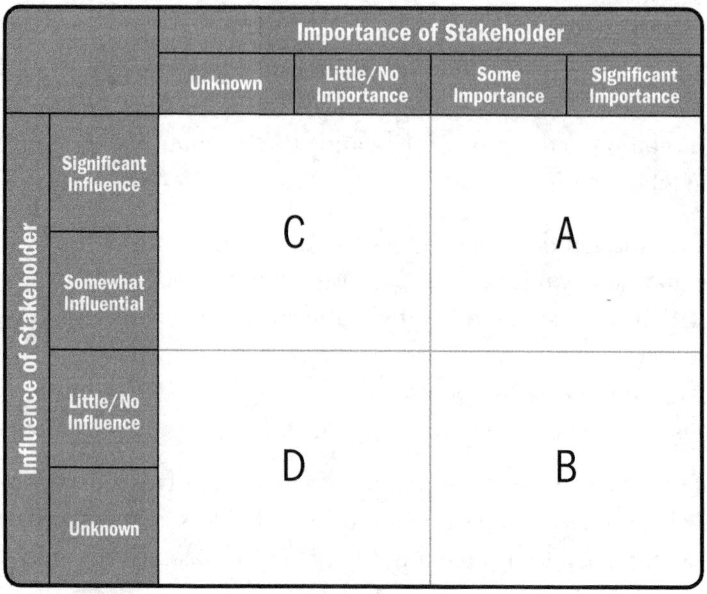

		Importance of Stakeholder			
		Unknown	Little/No Importance	Some Importance	Significant Importance
Influence of Stakeholder	Significant Influence	C		A	
	Somewhat Influential				
	Little/No Influence	D		B	
	Unknown				

Figure 6-5: Importance/influence model.

In addition to grid models, there are also onion models to categorize stakeholder influence and power.

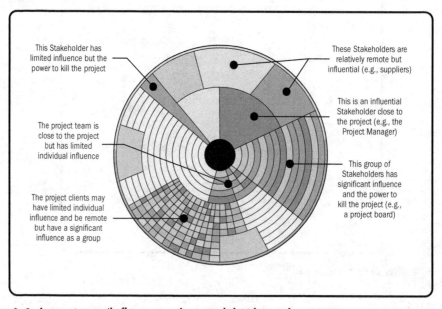

Figure 6-6: Importance/influence onion model (Alexander, 2005).

The project team and the project manager, based on their knowledge about the stakeholders and the organizational context, may assess power and influence of stakeholders. Considering that stakeholder management works with sensible information, it is very important to establish procedures and document classification.

Stakeholder information in the wrong hands may result in disasters. Imagine if a senior executive discovers that you have categorized him as an enemy of your project. . .

6.5 Step by Step

We've already stressed the importance of stakeholder involvement and engagement to project success. Now let's take a detailed look at stakeholder identification steps.

Stakeholder identification is a process that needs objectives and planning. You don't just go out there and try to discover who your stakeholders are to get all the information you can about them. You have to answer these questions:

- What do you need to know about each stakeholder? Do you need to gather more information about some of them?
- Where and how can you obtain the information?
- Who will have responsibility for gathering, analyzing, and interpreting the information?
- How and to whom will you distribute the information? Who will use or access information about stakeholders?

In this section, we are going to follow the approach suggested by (Wideman, quoted in Cleland et al., 2004):

1. Examine the Environment;
2. Determine the Type of Influence;
3. Categorize the Level of Influence; and
4. Use the Information Gathered.

As we know, stakeholder identification should occur as early as possible in the project and continue throughout its life. Likewise, the stakeholder analysis and strategy should be reviewed periodically throughout the project and updated as needed.

In fact, the first step proposed by (Wideman, quoted in Cleland et al., 2004) is stakeholders' identification. Here are some inputs to this process:

- Project charter;
- Statement of work;
- Contract;
- Procurement documents;

- Enterprise environmental factors; and
- Organizational process assets.

Stakeholder identification may use some of these tools and techniques:

- Stakeholder analysis;
- Expert judgment;
- Brainstorming;
- Organizational analysis;
- Templates and stakeholders breakdown structure;
- Review lessons learned and historical information; and
- Scope analysis.

It is important to examine the project environment and its context. Brainstorming and expert judgment are good techniques to identify individuals and groups who may be affected by the project or who can influence it. Stakeholders may be classified as internal or external.

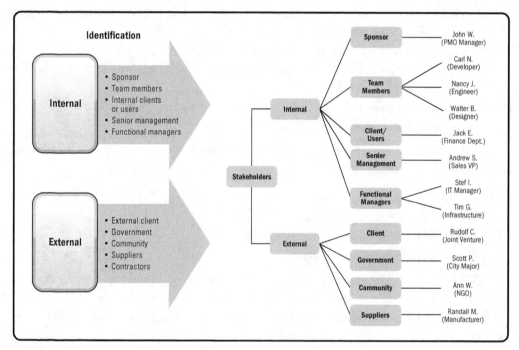

Figure 6-7: Stakeholders' identification.

One way to uncover stakeholders who you might not have thought about at the start is to ask known stakeholders if they're aware of anyone else who might be impacted by this project. Ask team members whether they're aware of stakeholders who haven't been identified.

Once you have a list of stakeholders, we can proceed to stakeholder analysis, which involves identifying the type of influence and categorization.

The second step proposed by Wideman (2004) is determining the type of influence, which can be done using the Salience model. This model involves three stakeholder aspects or attributes: power, urgency, and legitimacy. Power is related to a stakeholder's ability to change or influence the project. Urgency refers to a stakeholder's demand for attention (immediate, occasional, or rarely.) Legitimacy concerns the appropriateness of the stakeholder's participation at given times during the project.

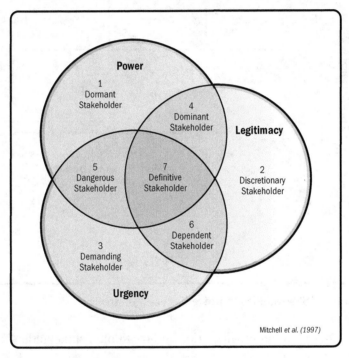

Figure 6-8: Salience model (Mitchell et al., 1997).

The Salience model defines seven types of stakeholders:

- Dormant stakeholders (power, no legitimacy and no urgency);
- Discretionary stakeholders (legitimacy, but no power and no urgency);
- Demanding stakeholders (urgency, but no legitimacy and no power);
- Dominant stakeholders (power and legitimacy, but no urgency);
- Dangerous stakeholders (power and urgency, but no legitimacy);
- Dependent stakeholders (legitimacy and urgency, but no power);
- Definite stakeholders (power, legitimacy and urgency); and
- Non-stakeholders (no power, no legitimacy and no urgency).

After determining types of stakeholder's influence, the next step (Wideman, 2004) is to categorize influences. We can use grid models like these:

- Power/interest grid,
- Power/influence grid, and
- Influence/impact grid.

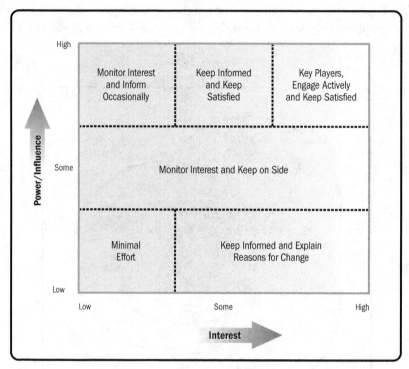

Figure 6-9: Example of strategies in power/interest matrix.

Influence categorization provides tips on how to plan stakeholders' management and which strategies to use.

As we follow these first steps (identify, classify type, and determine influence), we are gathering important information that will help us to build a solid communications plan and a solid stakeholders management plan.

If your organization usually manages multifaceted large projects, consider building an enterprise database (CRM – customer/stakeholder relationship management) linked to the project management software (EPM – enterprise project management). While helping individual projects in managing their stakeholders and storing information about them, this approach has another advantage in that it is possible to gather lessons learned and store historical information about stakeholders. Maybe, if you work frequently with some of your stakeholders, this will improve significantly your project performance.

Stakeholder management has to be systematized because it is a sensitive area, sometimes dealing with confidential information. You probably wouldn't like your stakeholders to know how you typified and categorized them. And you don't want them to know what strategies you're going to use to manage their expectations.

The last step proposed by Wideman (2004) concerns how we will use all that information. As I said before, we have a simple option of using spreadsheets or you can employ more sophisticated tools like databases and CRM software.

Table 6-4: Stakeholder registry updated.

Name	Role	Influence	Attitude	Priorities	Communication Needs	Strategy
Linda P.	Sponsor	High	Positive	ROI	Summary Reports	Keep Involved, Obtain Support
Howard H.	Technical Leader	High	positive	Quality	Weekly Meetings	Motivate
Martin S.	Supplier	Moderate	Neutral	Cost	Contract	Formal Communications
Susan E.	HR Manager	Low	Negative	Software Easy to Use	Meetings and Emails	Show Benefits of New System

In this step, using the stakeholder information gathered, we created the stakeholder management plan, which can be more detailed depending on your project. At the least, this plan has to cover these topics:

- Stakeholder information – collected in previous steps;
- Communication strategy – how to satisfy stakeholders' needs of accurate and relevant information in a timely fashion and using the right communication media;
- Engagement strategy – involve stakeholders in decisions, when pertinent, understanding their issues and needs; and
- Expectations management strategy – how to deal with positive and negative stakeholders, strategies to conflict solving, persuading and influencing, negotiation.

A stakeholder-commitment matrix (McElroy & Mills, 2003, quoted in Jepsen & Eskerod, 2008) can be used to understand each stakeholder's commitment to the project at a given moment compared to the type of commitment that the project manager finds is necessary or desirable for the project to be accomplished successfully. Possible types of commitment: active opposition, passive opposition, neutral, passive support, and active support. The type of commitment can be seen as a desired contribution (McElroy & Mills, 2003, quoted in Jepsen & Eskerod, 2008).

Stakeholder	Active Opposition	Passive Opposition	Neutral	Passive Support	Active Support
Suppliers			XO		
Top Management				X ⟶ ⟶ ⟶ O	
Colleagues in the Permanent Organization		X ⟶ ⟶ ⟶ ⟶ ⟶ ⟶ ⟶ O			
Grumbler				O ⟵ ⟵ ⟵ X	

X = Current Position, O = Necessary/Wanted Position

Figure 6-10: Example of stakeholder-commitment matrix (Jepsen & Eskerod, 2008, p. 337, Fig. 2).

An efficacious and efficient stakeholder management strategy includes a good communication strategy, which can greatly affect the stakeholder management, engagement, and expectations management. The right communication strategy should be based in engagement and expectations in a proactive and targeted approach.

Obtaining and evaluating feedback from stakeholders is also important to address issues and prevent conflicts. We are going to talk about how to build a solid communication plan and stakeholder management plan in Chapter 8.

6.6 Public Relations

Although we are not going to cover public relations in depth, it's an important topic to mention. Huge construction projects, involving public infrastructure or private facilities, have high potential impacts for a large spectrum of groups of stakeholders, such as these: government, environmentalists, and community.

Moreover, innovative intricate projects in pharmaceutical and medical areas can involve academic, religious people, and stakeholders mentioned previously. There can be different subgroups with conflicting interests among stakeholders, and there is always the possibility of hidden stakeholders also.

In cases when your project has to deal with large groups of people, it's better to have a public relations plan.

Public relations may be defined as a set of activities developed to improve the environment in which the project is executed, and hence improves its performance and lowers risk levels.

The public relations plan (PRP) will give direction and assign responsibilities for communication. An external image of the project and its benefits has to be built, while still handling critics and being honest about negative impacts. Of course, we will need a staff to undertake this effort of dealing with the public and media.

To succeed in public relations management, consider these steps:

- Know the objectives of your project and organization thoroughly;
- Identify and assess stakeholders, their influence, attitude, impact, and other characteristics;

- Define sensitive project areas and prioritize stakeholders' relative importance to the project;
- Plan actions to improve the perception of your company reputation and your project benefits;
- Public relations activities have to be planned and integrated with the project management plan, including resources; and
- Continuously monitor the effectiveness of public relations management during project execution, adjusting to manage stakeholders' expectations.

As you can imagine, a good PRP will promote better communications inside and outside the project.

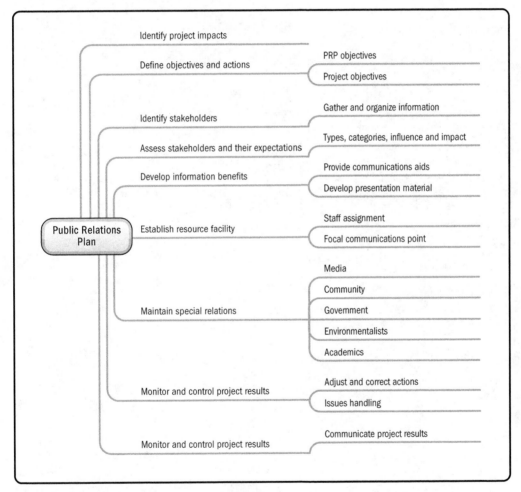

Figure 6-11: Public relations plan (mind map).

PRP prevents misunderstandings and misleading information. A golden rule is to be honest and transparent in public relations management. Again, don't forget that this plan has to be integrated with the entire project management plan.

Chapter 7

Managing Engagement and Expectations

All clients' needs and expectations are vastly different.

Bruce Bennett

7.1 Stakeholders' (Mind) Mapping

Contributions from a strong coalition of supportive and influential stakeholders are necessary to carry out a project successfully and it is the responsibility of the project manager to ensure such contributions through management of the stakeholders.

Always remember that stakeholder management needs purpose, you don't just go out there gathering information if you don't know if it will be useful. And never forget to define how stakeholder information will be used, stored and protected. Take care to prevent stakeholder information leakage, it could be disastrous.

Stakeholders: What Is On Their Minds?

Identifying stakeholders is the easy part of the job. Difficulties begin when we have to assess (sometimes guess) their expectations, needs, and agendas. We can say that satisfaction equals reality minus expectations.

$$Satisfaction = Reality - Expectations$$

In this chapter, we will finish the stakeholders' assessment and management plan. Then we will start executing the project, getting buy-in, managing expectations, and so on. We will see tools and techniques to collect requirements and to define project scope, after we define stakeholder management strategy.

Remember that we've already gathered enough information about stakeholders. Now we want to refine and detail important information. Drawing a mind map can help to understand not only who our stakeholders are, helping the project manager in visualization and communication, but also show interrelations and interactions among stakeholders.

Below we have some questions that can help direct stakeholder identification:

- Who is affected positively or negatively by the project?
- Who has power to make the project succeed or fail?
- Who has the money?
- Who has special skills needed by the project?
- Who can provide useful resources to the project?
- Who controls equipment or facilities that will be used by the project?
- Who influences the project's objectives?
- Who is responsible for permits, approval or licenses needed by the project?

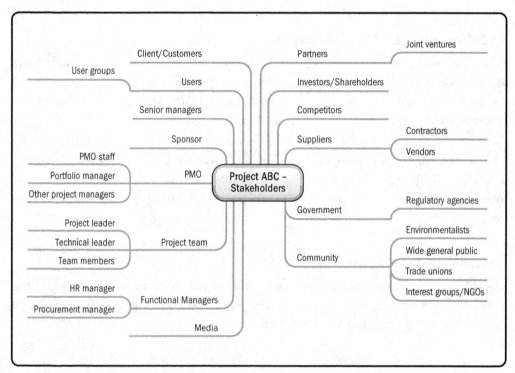

Figure 7-1: Stakeholders' mind mapping.

The challenge in stakeholder management is to create an environment for positive politics and foster win-win attitudes and open communication. Once you've identified them, it is time to gather more information about their preferences, needs, and expectations, so that you can categorize them and plan the stakeholder management strategy.

Table 7-1: Stakeholders' interest areas.

Stakeholder	Interest Area						
	Strategic Alignment	ROI	Legal and Regulations	Operational Changes	Cost	Technology	Quality
Functional Managers				•	•		•
Customers & Users					•		•
Suppliers & Contractors			•		•		
Team Members						•	•
Local Authorities			•	•			
Program Board	•	•	•	•	•	•	•
Senior Management	•	•		•			

If you cannot uncover what's on the stakeholders' minds, at least try to get all necessary clues. These are some sources:

- Other stakeholders,
- Business publications and media,
- Enterprise environmental factors,
- Organizational process assets, and
- Business partners, customers, and suppliers.

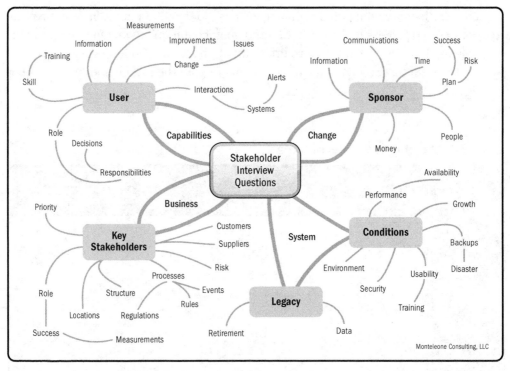

Figure 7-2: Mind map of generic questions for interviewing stakeholders (Monteleone, 2010).

A step further is to carry on stakeholders' sensitivity analysis and construct different scenarios to support our strategies. Some methodologies like problem structuring methods can help.

Table 7-2 defines strategies to manage stakeholders. Are they static?

It is important to understand that expectations are not steady, and stakeholders can change their minds about attitude (positive, negative). Mapping

Table 7-2: Influence/Importance matrix.

		Stake/Importance	
		Low	**High**
Influence/Power	**High**	**Dangerous:** Mitigate impacts, defend against	**Most Critical:** Collaborate with
	Low	**Least Priority:** Monitor or ignore	**Important Group:** Need of Empowerment, Involve

stakeholders' relationships and trying to infer how situations and circumstances could impact the project environment has to be done continuously during the project life cycle.

It is easier to understand levels of influence and power of groups of stakeholders when we know their relationships by mapping links of power and influence.

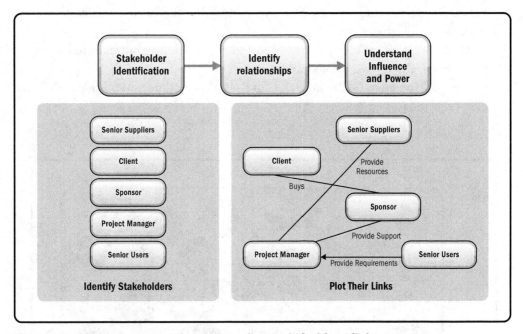

Figure 7-3: The importance of understanding stakeholders' links.

7.2 Stakeholders' Management

Tools and techniques seen until now offer different approaches to identify and classify individuals and groups of stakeholders. All the information gathered is used to develop strategies and plan stakeholders' management. However, sometimes when putting our plan into action, we find out that the consequences are far from what we've forecasted. Why? Because of politics.

It is said that Albert Einstein once observed that "Politics is more difficult than physics" (Englund & Bucero, 2006). Politics is a fact and will always be present. Englund and Bucero also said that a big pitfall for project managers is not taking the time to fully assess the political environment.

Although the identification of the social and political environment is very important, project managers face ethical dilemmas relating to explicitly categorizing stakeholders as negative towards the projects, especially when it came to singling out individuals (Cleland, 1986).

To help in understanding the political environment, Englund and Bucero (2006) compared stakeholders' characteristics to animals:

- Tiger: Solitary, powerful, strong, and skillful;
- Lion: Social, outgoing, approachable, loud;
- Bear: Solitary, intelligent, avoidant of people;
- Venomous snake: Cold-blooded, ruthless when provoked;
- Female black widow spider: Shy and solitary but poisonous, willing to devour weaker colleagues;
- Arctic fox: Easy to recognize but hard to catch; smiling but manipulative;
- Raccoon: Intensely curious; and
- Sheep: Dependent on the herd; willing to follow leaders and produce whatever is required.

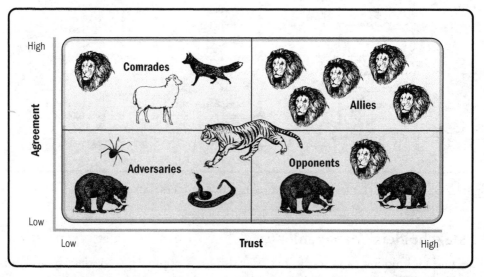

Figure 7-4: Stakeholder grid (*Project Sponsorship*, Englund & Bucero, 2006, p. 200 Used with permission.).

The "animals" describe the personal characteristics that need to be considered when deciding a course of action with each stakeholder to ensure support for a project. Start by reinforcing positions of strength, and then work on areas of concern.

The goal is trying to move stakeholders up and to the right on the stakeholder grid. And don't forget the possibility of hidden stakeholders. Use the knowledge about traits and behavior patterns to address each stakeholder's needs, as well as to protect yourself when necessary (Englund & Bucero, 2006).

Stakeholders' management, sometimes, is like nesting dolls[10]: there are many possibilities of finding a surprise inside. You have to find a balance between costs and benefits of stakeholders' management to define how much effort you'll put into it in each project.

Managing stakeholders along the project life cycle can be stressful for the project manager. It requires a huge effort in large involved projects. You can delegate part of this job and monitor its results using a spreadsheet, map, or even CRM software. It is a good practice to map stakeholders' management strategies along the project life cycle to keep them involved.

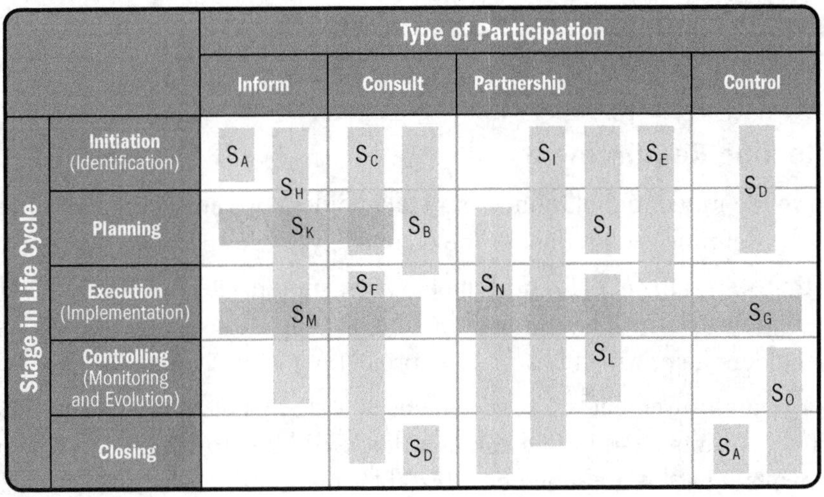

Stage in Life Cycle	Type of Participation			
	Inform	Consult	Partnership	Control
Initiation (Identification)	S_A S_H	S_C	S_I S_E	S_D
Planning	S_K	S_B	S_J	
Execution (Implementation)	S_M	S_F	S_N	S_G
Controlling (Monitoring and Evolution)			S_L	S_O
Closing		S_D		S_A

S_X = Stakeholder X

Figure 7-5: Stakeholder participation during the project life cycle.

A solid communications management plan will do the rest. In communications management, we can use the RACI matrix (Table 7-3), and we can make a communications matrix to define *who* will receive *what* information, *how* information will be delivered, and *when*.

---

[10] A Matryoshka doll is a Russian nesting doll that is a set of wooden dolls of decreasing size placed one inside the other.

Table 7-3: Stakeholder involvement using Microsoft Excel.

		Stakeholder						
		HR Manager	Supplier	County Dept	Client	Developers	Planning Staff	Project Manager
Activity/Phase	Develop Project Management Plan	C	I		I	I	R	A
	Assign Team Members	R, A				I	C	C
	Define Product Requirements		C	C	C	R	I	A

R = Responsible , A = Accountable , I = Inform , C = Consult

7.3 Collecting Requirements

Once we've identified and classified our stakeholders, we are ready to refine project planning by defining the product scope completely.

The first step is to collect requirements from appropriate stakeholders to find out what the real needs are. Then we will be able to propose solutions and choose, with the stakeholders help, which best fits the project objectives.

What is a requirement? A requirement is a statement that identifies characteristics or constraints desired in a solution that could be a product, service, or other. Requirements must be unambiguous, testable, measurable, and necessary for product acceptability.

Collecting requirements lead us to requirements engineering, a subset of systems engineering that involves activities devoted to identification of user requirements, analysis of the requirements to derive additional requirements, documentation of the requirements as a specification, and validation of the documented requirements against user needs (DoD, 1991).

Why do we bother so much with collecting requirements? First, they are the basis for scope definition. Moreover, bad requirements identification can lead to addressing the wrong problem, not satisfying stakeholders' needs, and this will result in project failure.

Although not thoroughly mentioned in the *PMBOK® Guide*, requirements and systems engineering are extremely important to most projects. The *PMBOK® Guide* is focused on project management-oriented processes, while we still employ huge effort in product-oriented processes. These product-oriented processes depend a lot on what kind of project we are developing, but systems engineering tries to bring a general approach of best practices in product, process, or service development.

By analyzing Figure 7-5, we can have a better perspective about the importance of requirements and systems engineering.

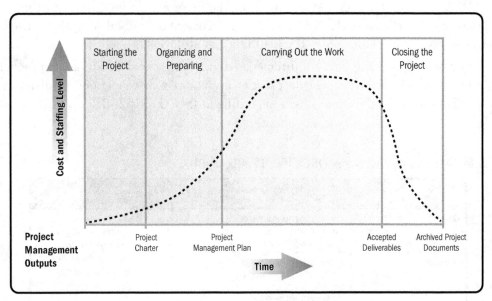

Figure 7-6: Project life cycle (Project Management Institute, 2008).

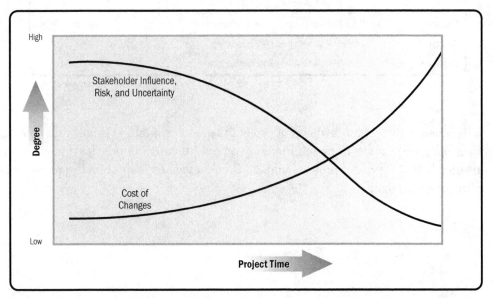

Figure 7-7: Stakeholder influence versus cost of changes (Project Management Institute, 2008).

Despite low cost and staff in initial project phases, it is here that we define and plan all subsequent work. In this sense, we can say that more than 70 % of a project budget is defined in earlier planning phases. That means requirements and scope are the basis for everything else in the project and we clearly need to invest time in doing it right.

I'd like to reinforce and stress the importance of an alliance between Project Management Institute (PMI) and INCOSE International Council of Systems Engineering (INCOSE). This is a strategic alliance at all levels.

Systems engineering and requirements engineering consider all of the product life cycle, which encompasses the product evolution from conception to disposal. Table 7-4 shows the life cycle stages according to ISO/IEC 15288.

Table 7-4: Life cycle stages (ISO/IEC 15288, 2008).

Life Cycle Stages	Purpose	Decision Gates
Concept	Identify stakeholders' needs Explore concepts Propose viable solutions	Decision Options: · Execute next stage · Continue this stage · Go to previous stage · Hold project activity · Terminate project
Development	Refine system requirements Create solution description Build system Verify and validate system	
Production	Mass produce system Inspect and test	
Utilization	Operational system to satisfy users' needs	
Support	Provide sustained system capability	
Retirement	Store, archive or dispose of the system	

Because of the comprehension of project management and systems engineering, project managers can work more efficiently by establishing boundaries and cooperation rules between project professionals to break a vicious loop of bad requirements leading to bad scope.

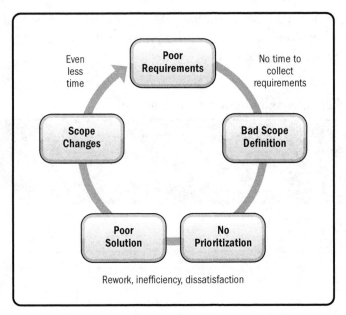

Figure 7-8: Vicious loop of poor requirements.

When collecting requirements, we start from the problem domain, where we draw a Statement of Needs from stakeholders' expectations. The Statement of Needs explains what the problem is and what the stakeholders would like to be capable of.

Then go to the solutions domain, where we derive solutions that address the Statement of Needs. We define high-level requirements that will be subsequently detailed in lower levels, subsystems, and components requirements.

The last thing to do is refined specifications, which means that we already have designed the system solution completely.

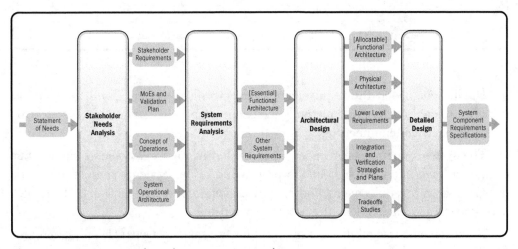

Figure 7-9: Systems engineering process overview.

Stakeholders will provide requirements. It is a good practice to define what is their necessary involvement and maybe separate them into classes of knowledge related to the system being developed.

Table 7-5: Stakeholder requirements contribution.

			Classes of Knowledge						
Stakeholder Role (The job title, department or organization that indicates a stakeholding)	Stakeholder Name (The name(s) of the responsible stakeholder(s))	Necessary Involvement (Estimate of when and how much time)	Goals	Business Constraints	Technical Constraints	Functionality	Look and Feel	Usability	Performance
Client									
Customer(s)									
Business/Subject Experts									
Future Ideas Specialists									
Current System Specialists									
Clerical User									
Technical User									
Potential User									
Sales Specialist									
Marketing Specialist									
Aesthetic Specialist									
Graphics Specialist									
Usability Specialist									
Safety Specialist									
Security Specialist									
Cultural Specialists									
Legal Specialists									
Environmental Specialists									
Maintenance Specialists									
Packaging Designer									
Manufacturer									
Product Installer									

Having completed the requirements and specifications, we build the solution using traditional engineering methods in specific knowledge areas, such as electronics and electrical engineering.

The systems engineering process represented in Figure 7-8 seems simple, but it takes a huge effort throughout the project life cycle. Systems engineering work doesn't end with requirements and specifications definition. The scope of product and project can change along the way toward closing.

Requirements traceability is important for two main reasons: (1) validation and (2) change control.

Validation assures that system requirements and specifications meet stakeholders' needs. The solution fits the problem. If you write great requirements that are not aligned with what is needed or what is proposed for the project, it will probably fail.

Requirements traceability is a powerful tool to validate requirements, but it also has a very important role in monitoring and controlling and in change control. Figure 7-10 shows low-level requirements must derive from high-level requirements, which creates linkages and dependencies. When receiving change requests, it's easier to analyze the impact of requirements and scope changes.

Best practices in requirements collecting, documenting, and controlling lowers project risk. Configuration and requirements management are critical success factors.

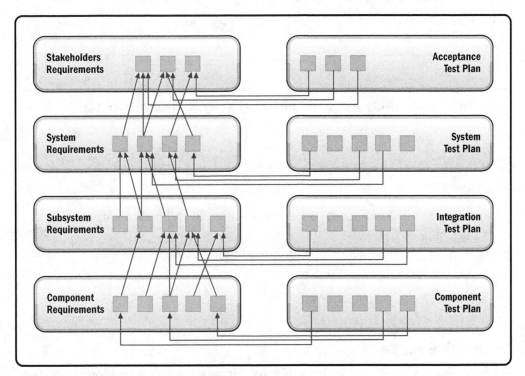

Figure 7-10: Requirements traceability (Hull, 2011, p. 14).

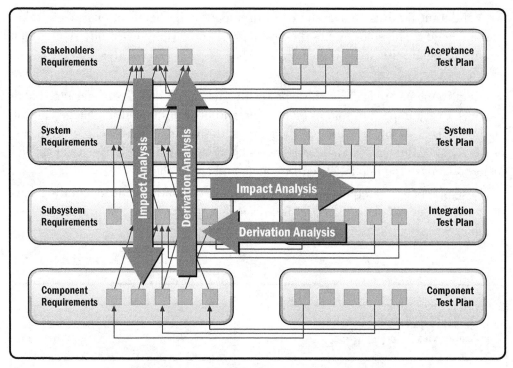

Figure 7-11: Requirements derivation and impact analysis (Hull, 2011, p. 15).

It's easy to realize that requirements are the basis for every project. There are many challenges:

- Understanding and capturing needs completely and unambiguously;
- Agreeing on tradeoffs;
- Documenting and communicating requirements; and
- Monitoring and controlling.

The next step is scope definition.

7.4 Defining Scope

Much of what was said in the previous topic already advanced on scope definition. Systems engineering encompasses requirements engineering. I'll show you once again the systems engineering process overview.

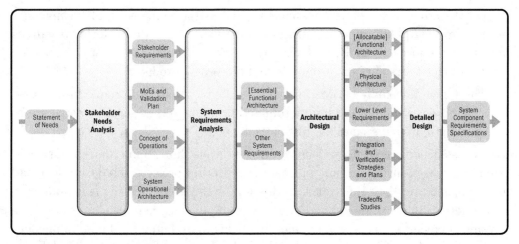

Figure 7-12: Systems engineering process overview.

This is already scope definition. We are defining product scope, which will drive project scope.

Thinking of scope, it is very important to involve the appropriate stakeholders in decisions. Complex selling—understanding, guiding, teaching, and persuading—factors in here. Understanding is about the problem and stakeholders' needs, as seen before.

However, we capture requirements from stakeholders, they are not experts. Usually, they have trouble determining the problem and what they want to get from the project. That means that needs will be stated in natural, non-jargon or technical language. The challenge to the project manager and his or her team is discovering and translating needs into requirements and specifications.

We do this by defining scope. Stakeholders have to be taught about possibilities and feasibility. If we go back to the previous paragraph and read it carefully, we can conclude that scope definition must be an iterative, incremental, and participative process. Stakeholders and team members will learn more by doing that and they will be able to refine and improve scope along the way.

Involving and engaging stakeholders are crucial parts of scope definition. When defining scope, stakeholders can get a taste of what they will get in the end of the project. The scope statement and the project plan document deliverables and its characteristics, showing also how the project will be carried on. From this point of view, scope definition is the first important project release.

In large multifaceted projects, as stated before, systems engineering plays an important role. It is a useful tool to support communications and stakeholders management, while still focusing on the product. That is, systems engineering is a product-oriented process.

On the other hand, project management is, as the name says, about management. It involves planning work to be done, organizing, and administering resources to achieve the project's goals. Systems engineering is about engineering or creating a new product with defining, designing, and building a product.

There is a dichotomy between project-oriented and product-oriented processes. Each of these areas has its own importance. Even though they seem to merge sometimes, we have to understand the role of each one.

In systems engineering, we focus on higher levels. It is an interdisciplinary field of engineering focusing on how intricate engineering projects should be designed and managed over their life cycles. In this way, systems engineering is a guide with best practices that can be applied to any system project. There is a transition from systems engineering to specific engineering fields in execution. Detailed implementation will be done using traditional tools, techniques, methods, and methodologies in different engineering knowledge areas.

Here we have the 10 commandments of good scope definition:

1. Involve and engage stakeholders;
2. Create a complete Statement of Needs;
3. Clearly understand the problem to be solved;
4. Diligently collect requirements;
5. Imagine and explore different solutions;
6. Ensure that the solution fixes the problem;
7. Define what is "good enough" (MoEs – Measures of Effectiveness);
8. Hold the team accountable for results; and
9. Make hard decisions, thoughtful tough decisions. Always monitor stakeholder expectation, get feedback, and hold the team accountable for results.

Chapter 8

Building a Solid Communications Plan

*There are no secrets to success. It is the result of preparation,
hard work and learning from failure.*

Colin Powell

8.1 The Communications Problem

Communication is not enough. You have to share and transfer information. Communications are usually reports, meetings, and emails, or something else. Project managers gather information they need to manage, monitor, and control the project. Then they identify stakeholders that need that information and send it to them. What is the problem with this approach?

Communicating is not throwing data, words, and reports to stakeholders or simply providing stakeholders easy access to information via software. This is a pushing approach, we feed stakeholders with information we want them to know. And that's a big mistake, which results in poor communication.

Miscommunication is the norm in many organizations. It is not different in project management (Stacey, 2000, quoted in Appelo, 2011, p. 253). There are many surveys connecting poor communications to project failure, some of them concluded that communication's problems are the main cause of project failure (IT Cortex, n.d.).

Communicating is difficult because it involves encoding and decoding, which are impacted by personal filters and perceptions. When I say something, you can understand another thing because of your background, preferences, and more. Moreover, there are two other problems: noise and channel. Which channel we choose can influence how information will be accepted. For example, a message sent from formal channels is different from the same message communicated in an informal talk.

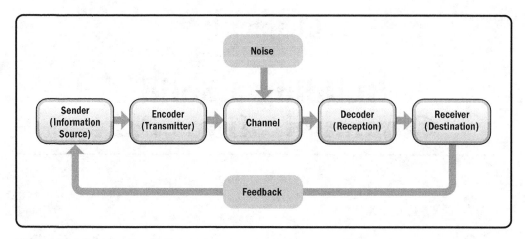

Figure 8-1: Communication process.

Traditional communication process, sometimes, doesn't include feedback, that is, the sender (or source) pushes information to the receiver without caring about how it's getting there, how it's going to be decoded, or understood. Including feedback creates two-way communication, which allows the sender and the receiver to confirm and check information exchanged.

Going beyond traditional communication, Appelo (2010) introduced the concept of relationship in communications. He described communication as a phenomenon constituted by information, relationships and feedback. That's what we've been talking about in this book.

Information is merely the passive object of communication. The real process involves relationship, because only people can communicate, objects can't. I believe that the communication process ends with the receiver, when he or she understands the information that the sender sent. But how do we know if the receiver understood exactly what the sender wanted? Feedback.

Feedback completes the communication process, or phenomenon, and reinforces relationships, helping build trust and avoid miscommunication. Mersino (2007) says that feedback is the breakfast of champions.

From that, we can infer that poor communication is frequently an effect of bad relationships, which are the real cause, and why engaging and involving stakeholders is so important in initiation and throughout the project life cycle.

Although information is the object, it is not less important than building relationships, getting, and providing good feedback. If you don't have good information, why would anybody want to hear you? To gather valuable information, the project manager has to be proactive, using all formal and informal ways of collecting it. Moreover, from the project management point of view, it is important to monitor and control the project, which also involves collecting, analyzing, storing, and reporting information appropriately.

Robert Mai and Alan Akerson (2003) in The Leader as a Communicator provided these three main roles for leaders:

- Community builder: meaning-maker, storyteller, and trust builder;
- Navigator: direction setter, transition pilot, and linking agent; and
- Renewal champion: critic, advocate, and coach.

These roles can be played together, and the leader can adapt his approach depending on the context, like in situational leadership (Hersey & Blanchard, 1977).

For me, these roles are fantastic for summarizing what we expect from leaders. And the project manager is a leader and has to act like one. Leaders as communicators is a very insightful comparison.

You can't communicate without these:

- Relationship building (trust builder),
- Good information (meaning-maker), and
- Nice talk (storyteller).

For me, building relationships is one of the most important aspects of being a project manager. Project managers do not do the job; they get the job done through team members and other stakeholders. Consequently, stakeholders' management is about creating an environment, so stakeholders could make the most significant contribution they were capable of making to the project.

Much of what was said on this topic is restricted to one-to-one communication. However, the project manager has to care about understanding and influencing communication between stakeholders. The more stakeholders we have, the more communication channels or relationships have to be built.

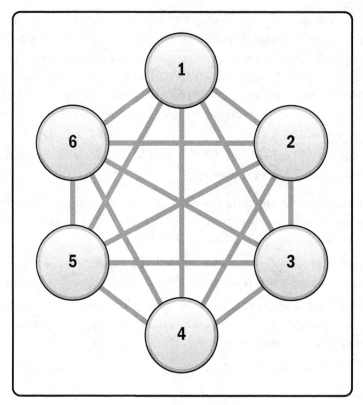

Figure 8-2: Communication channels and stakeholders.

We talked about the importance of communication and its crucial aspects; however, project managers have to care about many stakeholders. That is, they have to build multi-relationships from them to others, (one-to-many) and they have to shape or influence communication among stakeholders (many-to-many), while stimulating project supporters and helping to disseminate the right information.

Karen Stephenson (2005, quoted in Appelo, 2011), identified three archetypes of communicators in a social network:

- Hubs are people who draw information to themselves and then broadcast it all around them.
- Gatekeepers are experts at carefully managing information flows, knowing what to say to whom, and what not (to say).
- Pulse takers are great observers of people and trends, being excellent mentors and coaches.

Given the diversity of stakeholders, communication ends up being the key to obtaining project support. Identifying relationships and archetypes in communication networks helps the project manager to be more effective.

Sometimes, in projects, the fact that the majority of team members and other stakeholders, all with different backgrounds, may have not worked together before creates another challenge to the project manager: team growing, relationships fostering, and trust building.

One way to overcome this problem is to set directions upfront, so there is no doubt who is the point of contact in the project. The project manager can delegate to another team member the role of primary information source or point of contact. This approach helps in creating and reinforcing project governance.

Standards and procedures have to be written and shared, so every stakeholder knows the rules of the game. Also, reviews and technical exchange meetings should be held on a continuous basis. General announcements and information have to be frequently released; you can use a website, blackboard, or any other channel that fits your needs.

Once the project manager sets consistent and continuous communication procedures, then stakeholders start to become reliant on the information provided. Stakeholders won't need to look for other sources of competing and conflicting information.

All project information comes in and goes out through the point of contact, which can be a team member or group delegated by the project manager. Following this advice will foster a stable and trustworthy environment. And remember, people don't feel comfortable with uncertain and always changing situations.

8.2 Communicating Efficiently

According to the previous topic, project managers have to be something like the leader as a navigator. He is the captain of the boat. Project managers have to balance their behavior as a leader setting directions and inspiring, and as a manager to organize and control the project's tasks and resources.

As you know, the first step to building a solid communications plan is stakeholders' identification through any tools and techniques mentioned in Chapter 7. Once stakeholders are identified, you have to talk to them and map their information needs.

As part of the stakeholders' assessment, you can group, classify, and analyze them. Use some models like power/influence or the Salience model. These graphical views of stakeholders help you in grouping and categorizing them. Key project stakeholders need further assessment to deeply understand their needs and expectations. Here are some questions you can ask yourself that may help you in creating the communications management plan:

- Do my stakeholders demand formal or informal communication?
- Do they prefer face-to-face, telephone, or written communication?

- With which communication tools are stakeholders comfortable (email, video-conferencing, Enterprise Project Management software, etc)?
- How does reporting generally occur in both my organization and in the client's organization? What is the communications flow?
- What do reports look like in my organization and in the client's organization? Are there templates that should be observed?
- What is the reporting relationship between the stakeholders? How does hierarchy work in the project's environment?

The right communication strategy includes delivering the needed information to the right stakeholder at the right time, and using an appropriate communication tool. Table 8-1 shows another simplified example.

Table 8-1: Communications matrix.

Event (Trigger)	Documents (What)	Responsible (Sender)	Stakeholders (Receivers)	Media (How)	Periodicity (When)
Sponsorship Meeting	Meeting Agenda Project Charter	Project Manager	Sponsor	Form	Initiating (01 meeting)
Client Meeting	Meeting Agenda Project Charter	Project Manager	Sponsor Client	Form	Initiating (01 meeting)
Project Management Presentation	Meeting Agenda Preliminary Project Plan	Project Manager	Sponsor Client	PowerPoint Presentation Meeting Agenda	Initiating (01 meeting)
Kickoff Meeting	Meeting Agenda Preliminary Project Plan Project Objectives	Project Manager	Project Team	PowerPoint Presentation	Initiating (01 meeting)
Requirements Definition	Preliminary Scope Statement Requirements Management Plan Requirements Documents	Project Manager	Project Team	Form	Planning - Collecting Requirements (05 meetings)
Project Scope Statement Definition	Project Scope Statement Requirements Documents Preliminary Project Plan	Project Manager	Project Team	Form	Planning - Scope Definition (03 meetings)
Requirements Validation	Project Scope Statement Requirements Documents Preliminary Project Plan	Project Manager	Sponsor Client	PowerPoint Presentation Meeting Agenda	Planning - Requirements and Scope Validation (02 meetings)
Project Management Plan Definition	Meeting Agenda Project Management Plan	Project Manager	Project Team	PowerPoint Presentation Form	Planning - Project Management Plan (weekly meetings)
Project Execution	Project Management Plan Assignments RACI Matrix	Project Manager	Project Team	Form	Execution
Project Monitoring and Controlling	Project Management Plan Project Information Performance Reports Issues Register	Project Manager	Sponsor Project Team	PowerPoint Presentation Form	Monitoring and Controlling (weekly meetings)
Project Review (client)	Project Management Plan Project Information Performance Reports Issues Register	Project Manager	Sponsor Client	Form	Milestones
Project Closing	Lessons Learned Meeting Agenda Final Report	Project Manager	Project Team	Form	Closing
Project Closing (client)	Meeting Agenda Final Report	Project Manager	Sponsor Client	Form	Closing

To successfully manage stakeholders and communications, we have to be proactive. On the other hand, no matter how hard we try to involve and engage stakeholders, they probably are busy people whose attention is difficult to capture. Without engagement, important issues might be overlooked.

To mitigate this problem, focus on what each stakeholder would want to know. Try to imagine how stakeholders would be affected by project results and project changes.

One of the secrets of good communication is to divide it into small chunks, so that the receiver/stakeholder can bite at it, that is, read it and understand it. Periodicity is another essential aspect of communication. Don't let your project be "forgotten" by stakeholders because you are not communicating frequently.

Actually, the ultimate purpose is to reduce the amount of communication and coordination necessary to the project. Stakeholders will benefit because they will have only relevant information, and they won't be flooded with unnecessary data. From the project manager's point of view, that's also good because he or she will spend less energy communicating efficiently.

There is a big problem that I have not mentioned until now: informal communication network around the project. Even if you establish a hierarchical and authoritative structure in your project, or in your organization, information invariably flows through an informal network of communication. You don't have to worry about stopping or prohibiting this kind of communication, you have to take actions to ensure that trustful information flows.

To cope with that, project managers can't be shy. They have to create and implement standard methodology and project management processes. The project managers have to grow a project culture aligned with project governance. Once stakeholders are familiar with standards, they will use it and hold one another accountable for using it, reinforcing governance.

Project managers will be the master authoritative information source in the project. They need to know what is happening to take action. If they notice a lack of information, ambiguity, or unclear issues, project managers have to take the initiative to improve it. Of course, the sponsor is also essential to the project success. One of the key sponsor roles is to assign authority and responsibility to the project manager by visible demonstrations that strengthen the project manager's power and legitimacy.

In summary, communication and stakeholder management involves four basic steps:

- Identify the key stakeholders, map their needs and expectations, and create a strategy so that they are aware of and supportive of the project. Involve and engage them.
- Communicate to the stakeholders a clear vision of the project, specific objectives, and resources required. Ask for feedback to ensure comprehension.

- Ensure stakeholders participation, contribution, ownership and support while planning the project. Create a solid communication plan to give each stakeholder the information they need, and don't waste their time with non-relevant data.
- Plan execution and implementation, keeping in touch with stakeholders. Inform them periodically.
- Obtain and evaluate feedback from stakeholders and address their issues.

8.3 Project Communication Step by Step

Planning communications, as in planning stakeholders' management, is something tricky. In stakeholders' management, you have to discover (identify) all stakeholders, unveil (bring out and document) their needs, and guess (unveil) their expectations. Communications management also involves dealing with people, expectations, conflicts, and complexity.

Table 8-2: Example of stakeholder registry, including stakeholder management strategy.

Stakeholder	Goals, Motivations, and Interests	Power and Influence	Importance to and Impact on Project	Role on Project	Win-Win Strategies

Stakeholders and communications management are ongoing processes. Remember that some people say that the project managers spend 90% of their time communicating? So, you've gotta plan for it.

Communications Planning

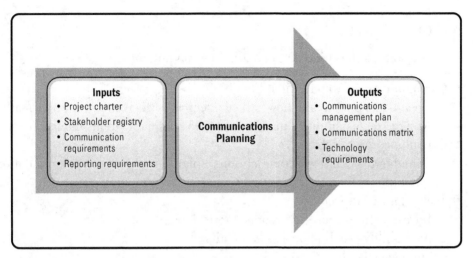

Figure 8-3: Communications management planning.

The communications plan has to answer who needs what information, when they need it, and how it will be delivered (Phillips, 2009). We started from these inputs:

- Project Charter
  - o Project objectives and scope
  - o Deliverables, milestones, and estimates
- Stakeholders' Registry
  - o Client, users, sponsor
  - o Project team
  - o Vendors, suppliers, contractors
  - o Functional managers
  - o Other stakeholders
- Communications Requirements
  - o Who needs what information and why?
  - o When do they need information?
  - o How information will be delivered?
  - o Who will relay the information to whom?

- Reporting Requirements
  - o Status and variances
  - o Performance
  - o Issues and risks
  - o Other attributes

Then we process these inputs to obtain these outputs:

- Communications Management Plan
  - o Documents and details how stakeholders will receive relevant information
  - o Assigns responsibilities and resources to communications management
- Communications Matrix
  - o Summarizes the communications plan, including communications schedule
- Technology Requirements
  - o Infrastructure—meeting rooms, for example
  - o Availability—cell phones, fax, emails
  - o Storage—database
  - o Release—website, for example
  - o Distribute—reports
  - o Team management—other tools

Table 8-3: Example of a communications matrix.

Stakeholder	Reports to Recieve (Scope of Interest)	Amount of Detail	Best Formatting Format	Frequency of Reporting	Delivery Mechanism

Information Distribution

It is important to establish a focal point, a single authoritative information source to the project. Stakeholders will rely on this source, and they will come to it when they want to know something else. This reduces conflicting information and rumors, which can poison your project.

It is clear that the project manager has to be proactive. However, this doesn't prohibit him or her from delegating. In large multifaceted projects, the project manager focuses on key stakeholders and delegates to other team members the communication with other stakeholders.

Information gathering and data collecting can't be done by the project manager; you won't have time to do it. But the project manager oversees and ensures information validity.

Once we have the communications plan, distributing information includes these:

- Collecting and storing information appropriately
  o Use technology to make it easier
  o Schedule and budget
  o Scope, changes, and milestones
  o Risks and issues
- Analyzing information
  o Risk analysis, performance
  o Change requests
  o Other information
- Providing reports
  o Standard reports
  o Custom reports
  o Team communications

Table 8-4: Example of a detailed communications matrix.

Type of Stakeholder	Content of Reports	Format	Frequency	Distribution Method
• Executive or strategist	• Outcomes • Major successes • Major problems with solutions	• Color • Charts with graphics • Brief • Use few words	• Monthly • Quarterly	• Hard copy via courier or face-to-face meeting
• Project team member (from your organization and client organization)	• Status of tasks • Open issues • Resources needed	• Bullet-list style • Supporting, detailed documents, if needed	• Weekly • Bi-weekly	• Email • Fax • During project status meeting
• Other stakeholders	• Status of project • Key successes • Outcomes	• Short articles or stories	• Monthly	• Place in organizational communication documents, such as newsletters and news briefs

Communications management is not only about outbound information but also about inbound information. Consider all the emails, phone calls, queries, and sticky notes you receive every day concerning your project.

It's necessary to distinguish when you need formal communication. Important information should be stored and documented as part of your information management system. You may need it for future reference and lessons learned. Maybe you'll have harder issues like change management and stakeholders' issues to solve based on previous information exchanged.

Although reports are one of the most common ways of sharing a project's information, communications can benefit a lot from using other formats like dashboards. Customization helps in delivering the right information in a more pleasant format and adds value both to communications management and stakeholder engagement.

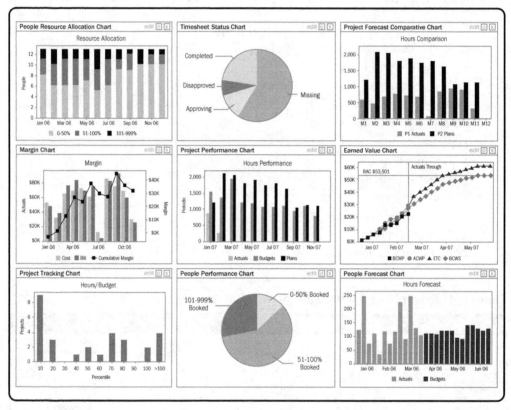

Figure 8-4: Examples of dashboards.

Infographics is a growing area of study. Kerzner (2001) defends the involvement of designers and information specialists in projects to help devise good communications strategies and to provide visual aid to share information with efficacy and efficiency.

Communications in Acquisitions Management

Although acquisitions management and procurement represents another knowledge area for the *PMBOK® Guide*, it's easy to see that it has a lot to do with communications.

Communicating with sellers, suppliers, and subcontractors differs from dealing with a given organization. That's because we need more formal communication with external stakeholders, especially when there are legal implications and contracts.

It's difficult to create generalizations about this topic because there can be plenty of different procurement procedures. I can't give you a step-by-step methodology here. But I can advise you on some common practices:

- Request seller responses
  o As a project manager, you may or may not be involved here. It's important that you create complete specifications, requirements, and statements of work for what you want to buy.
- Selecting sellers
  o Provide objective criteria for two reasons: (1) You want to buy the best stuff; and (2) If you give ambiguous or incomplete criteria, you may even be prosecuted by sellers if they think that they were damaged.
- Contract administration
  o As a project manager, you'll probably have legal support in contracts. But contract administration is usually assigned to the project manager. You have to assure that vendors are following what's prescribed in the contract. If something is wrong, you have to communicate with the vendor formally, and you may also communicate legal or procurement departments in your organization.
- Screening systems, and determinations that help determine which vendor

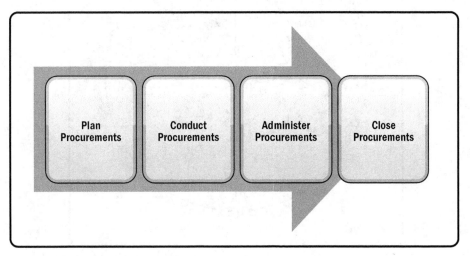

Figure 8-5: Procurement management.

Sometimes, the process is not straightforward. Depending on what you're buying, there can be lots of negotiation. Imagine that you are managing a large intricate aerospace project. You are going to contract some subsystems for it. This kind of acquisition involves more of a partnership between seller and buyer than a simple sale.

Monitoring Communications Management

As any other area in project management, it's important to review communication results. Feedback plays a major role here, but we have to go beyond it.

Communication efficiency and efficacy have to be assessed qualitatively or quantitatively to improve it along the way.

Monitoring and controlling communications is strictly related to managing stakeholders' expectations. You'll have to adapt your strategy depending on the environment and circumstances.

As a project manager, you have to seek out communication opportunities to obtain support, lookout for communication barriers to deal with, and find communication gaps or improvement opportunities.

It's a non-stop process (Plan-Do-Check-Act). If there is a project, communication is there through the entire life cycle. And it's your job to optimize communications in the project.

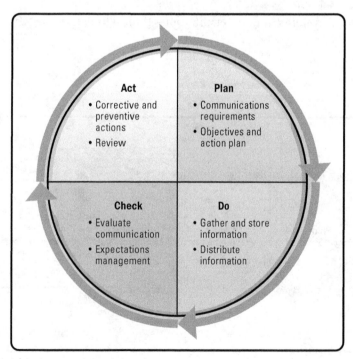

Figure 8-6: Communications management.

Efficiency

Concluding, you're not a courier. You're not an expeditor. You are a manager, the project manager. Planning and making it happen is your job. Delegation has to be part of your daily work. You also have to know how to use technology, tools, and techniques to do your job efficiently.

Chapter 9

Getting Buy-in

Until one is committed, there is hesitancy,
the chance to draw back, always ineffectiveness.

Johann Wolfgang von Goethe

9.1 Learning

In a project, support or buy-in is like the air you breathe. Without it, your project will die. And to get buy-in, you have to identify stakeholders, learn about them by stakeholder analysis and information gathering, develop and implement stakeholder engagement strategies.

It's incredible that project managers are always worried about internal achievements of their projects and about internal project management—without paying attention to the external project environment.

Some of us are afraid of politics. But, to be effective, project managers and their sponsors need to learn how to thrive in a political environment (Englund & Bucero, 2006, p. 172). It's not an option, especially in large intricate projects; you have to become politically sensitive.

Most of the time, project managers are worried about negative stakeholders, and they forget to strengthen positive stakeholders. A major project killer is blank out, not resistance. In other words, when project managers are not effective in communicating with and engaging stakeholders, they stop paying attention to the project and forget about it. Your project will lose support, sink to a low priority, and die of starvation.

When dealing with stakeholders, there is a joke that says, "If you don't explain, they are not going to understand the project. If you explain, they are not going to understand it either..."

Although a joke, there is truth behind it. Most of the stakeholders can't understand project details because they have other interests and needs.

A chief financial officer (CFO), for example, probably has no idea about aircraft aerodynamics, but the CEO holds the budget. So you'd better speak his or her language to show how important your project is, if you want some money.

Although different stakeholders have specific demands, expectations and interests, there usually are common issues.

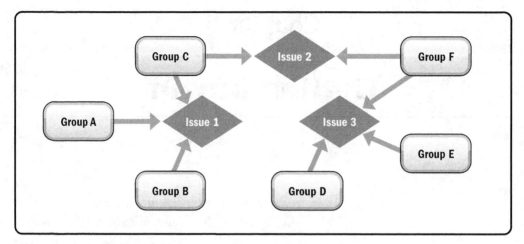

Figure 9-1: Identifying common issues among stakeholders' groups.

The identification of these issues is very helpful, providing better resource allocation to satisfy key stakeholders and groups of stakeholders by attacking foundational issues or common areas of concern to key stakeholders of the project.

In this chapter, we have interesting tools and techniques. Once you've identified stakeholders and mapped their expectations and needs, you can define your communications strategy. But how can you guarantee stakeholders' support? Try using a complex sales approach and soft problem-structuring methods.

The complex sales approach will be reviewed in the next topic about persuasion.

As managing projects is becoming more multifaceted, there has been an increasing interest in connecting problem-structuring methodologies with project management. (Howick & Eden, 2001; Winter, 2006; Davis, MacDonald & White, 2010).

9.2 Soft Systems Methodology

The Soft Systems Methodology (SSM)(Checkland, 1999) is a problem-structuring method particularly well suited to messy project situations (Checkland & Winter, 2005). SSM emphasizes problematical situations, conflicts, and multiperspectives. SSM is a methodology to learn about the problematical situation, while defining it.

SSM focuses on soft problems—problems not clearly defined. Often it is an area of concern that enables decision opportunities. This methodology enables stakeholders to embark on a process of learning about the real situation being investigated from different points of view, while simultaneously seeking to structure the problem within the paradigm of systems thinking. As a result, alternatives and solutions might appear, improving the problem situation itself.

Considering that a project implies the exercise of a combination of engineering and management skills, Checkland (1975) argued that it is necessary to use systems analysis as a process of conscious inquiry to understand multidimensional projects as a whole. Gardiner (2005) also supported that project management can be studied more effectively using systems theory and systems thinking because of their analytical and holistic approach.

Checkland (1981) identified seven stages in SSM as shown in Figure 9-2.

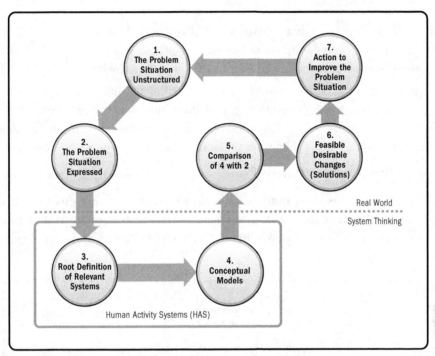

Figure 9-2: Soft Systems Methodology (Adapted from Checkland, 1981, Fig. 6).

SSM stages explained:

1. Problem situation unstructured: area of concern, purpose, or end-objectives.
2. Problem situation expressed: rich picture created to represent pictorially the problem situation. The rich picture describes the structure and processes of the problem situation.
3. Root definition: clarifies what needs to be addressed and which human activity system is of concern. You can have more than one root definition, representing the HAS (Human Activity Systems)
4. Conceptual models: use creativity and logical argument to derive relevant activities in the human activity system and build conceptual models in different levels of abstraction.
5. Comparing 4 to 2 (real world and the conceptual model): provide comments and recommendations
6. Identify feasible solutions: you can use a multi-criteria model to compare alternatives
7. Improve the problem situation: implement the solution

Winter (2006) summarized four core principles to the SSM learning cycle:

- Find out about the situation, including the cultural and political aspects.
- Formulate some relevant models of purposeful activity for discussion.
- Discuss the situation using the models and seek accommodations.
- Take action to improve the situation.

Although we are not going to explore SSM further, I encourage you to research about this important topic. Our objective now is only to show a model that can integrate multi-stakeholders' perspectives into the project as a whole.

As project managers, we benefit from problem-structuring methods, especially soft approaches like SSM, by engaging and involving stakeholders proactively in a learning process about project definition and planning. We are going to finish with a simple example of SSM in project management.

Project: **Build a New Power Plant**

1. Problem situation unstructured: *We don't have enough energy supply*.
2. Problem situation expressed: A rich picture contains both appropriate symbols for real world activities and words and is an attempt to express the area of concern.

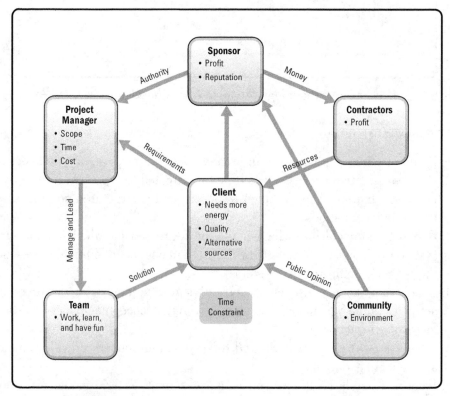

Figure 9-3: Simplified rich picture for the project "Build Power Plant."

3. Root definition: The purpose of the project is not building a new power plant as initially stated, the end-objective is that the client has enough energy. The client expresses the most important HAS (human activity system) to be further studied. We could define more than one root definition to represent different HAS. For each HAS, we have a CATWOE analysis.

Root definition (RD): to ensure that the client has enough energy

CATWOE Analysis
    Customer: client
    Actors: sponsor, project manager, team, and contractors
    Transformation: provide enough energy
    Weltanshauung: energy fuels operations
    Owner: client
    Environment: client environment

4. Conceptual models: We could develop many models in different levels to better understand the problem. Simplifying, I've created a conceptual model of how the client uses energy, based on the root definition stated before.

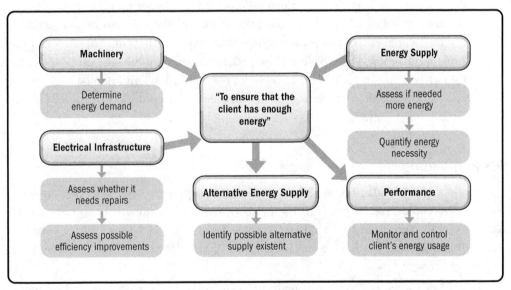

Figure 9-4: Conceptual model based on Root Definition "to ensure that the client has enough energy."

5. Comparison between conceptual models and the real world. This stage compares what we are now to what we want to be able to do. The conceptual model (or models) represents how things should work. The reality has to be changed in some way to improve the problem-situation.

Table 9-1: Comparison to reality.

Activity (In the conceptual model)	Exist or not (In real world)	Present Mechanism	Measures of Performance	Recommendations	Comments
Determine machinery energy demand	In part	Old machinery doesn't have manuals	None	Use energy meters to determine individual energy demand	Urgent
Assess electrical infrastructure for repairs	In part	Repairs are made when energy problems happen	None	Implement preventive maintenance	Create performance measurements
Assess electrical infrastructure for efficiency improvements	No	None	None	Contact vendors or consultants and ask for diagnosis	
Assess energy supply	Yes	Energy meter	Contract with electrical company	Improve	Urgent
Quantify total energy needed	No	None	None	Create a time curve for energy usage	
Monitor and control machinery performance	In part	Corrective maintenance	None	Implement preventive maintenance	
Identify alternative energy supply	No	None	None	Search for alternative energy suppliers	

6. Feasible desirable changes: project manager and his team propose solutions (project scope). In stage 5, we compare the ideal conceptual model to reality, so that we can propose feasible solutions and create action plans.

7. Implement solutions: project execution. Actually, the solution implementation might encompass all the project's life cycle. Stages 1 to 6 may happen prior to project initiation. Once we have the problem statement and the proposed solution aligned strategically to stakeholders' expectations and needs, we can use our traditional project management knowledge, as compiled in the *PMBOK® Guide*, for example.

9.3 Persuading

Using tools and techniques to define and plan the project with help and involvement of stakeholders solves part of the project manager's problem. The project manager needs to transform that rich picture created in the last topic into a cohesive project management plan. This implies the solution definition, which leads us back to project scope.

Using brainstorming tools and techniques to collect requirements and problem-structuring methods was in the problem domain. The problem domain represents the context and purpose of a project, and delimitates its objectives and values. Once we understand the problem, it's the project manager's and the project manager's team's role to design a solution.

In the solution domain, the project team is going to propose and analyze alternatives and strategies to the project. Costs and benefits have to be clearly stated so that stakeholders can make informed decisions.

Getting stakeholders' agreement is not easy. But you have to do all that you can to make it happen in project initiation. When a project starts, we are in a honeymoon phase. Everybody is excited and collaboratively engaged.

With an agreement on scope in the beginning of the project, you'll probably never get it! As time goes on, new expectations and conflicts arise, making agreements more difficult.

Acting as a seller, the project manager has to be proactively persuasive. Building a guiding coalition of influential stakeholders who support the project is mandatory. This support or its lack represents a powerful force either toward or away from the goal.

It is the project manager's responsibility to clarify and understand the project's objectives. The project manager also identifies key stakeholders and works with them to determine the project scope.

Actually, not everybody will be happy with your project. That's an illusion. However, you have to ensure that key stakeholders are supportive by building coalitions to stand up for your project. First, focus your efforts on persuading key stakeholders, then you can extend your circles of influence and power to get more support.

9.4 Motivating

Show me how people are measured and I'll show you how they behave. Have you ever heard that? There is also the reverse: If it's not measured, nobody does it.

We are all human, with our personal aspirations and motivation. However, we are not only directed by rewards and punishments but also by values.

Values are deep-rooted beliefs that govern our conscience like inner voices that reflect values and beliefs. We feel uncomfortable with other people and organizations who act against our beliefs.

Motivational theories are mainly divided into two groups. One group believes that motivation is intrinsic to individuals and that all we can do is provide an environment that doesn't demotivate them. On the other hand, the other groups firmly believe that individuals are driven by external motivators, which can be positive (rewards) or negative (punishments).

Of course, some motivational approaches try to balance internal and external motivators to better catch the individual's reality.

For now, we are not interested in individual motivation. We want to understand stakeholders' motivation as a group. To enhance stakeholders' propensity to support the project objectives, the project manager cannot commit integrity crimes because they destroy trust and blow away stakeholders' commitment.

Motivating is intrinsically tied to persuading. Daniel Pink (2011) identifies different driving forces that motivate people. He says that we are not more tied to the old carrot-and-stick notion. Pink defends an obvious concept of self-actualization, that was present even in Maslow's hierarchy of needs. The top of the pyramid is the strongest motivating driving force.

People want to make a difference. People want to be part of great achievements. An irrefutable proof is recreational sports and other voluntary groups and associations that we engage in. Why do we do that? Self-actualization.

Another important aspect of motivation is feedback. Pink (2011) says that organizations create feedback deserts. This is a big problem, because we've already seen that feedback is the champion's breakfast (Mersino, 2007).

Feedback is so paramount that organizations are trying to gamify the way their employees work and also trying to gamify users' experiences. Why? Feedback. People play games not only because they are fun but also because there is a score, a metric to instantly progress toward your goal.

This is the environment project managers have to create in their projects through collaborative work and stakeholders' engagement. Jane McGonigal (2011) is another firm believer that gaming engages and motivates people.

All of this sounds pretty good, right? You might be asking yourself "But how do I do that?" or "How can I create that environment?" There is no standard recipe. However, concerning project management, we can use a methodology to generate buy-in. Once you have identified key stakeholders and their expectations, follow these steps:

- Establish a strategic storyline for your project
  - The Project Charter has essential project information and is a very important document to start the project. You can use it as a basis to envision the big picture of your project according to its objectives.
    - Cast a positive vision of future appealing to your stakeholders
    - Clarify a project's objectives and stay focused
    - The project manager has to know what the definition of success for the project to define what is "good enough"
- Engage stakeholders
  - How will your stakeholders' agenda be addressed by your project?
  - Create the stakeholders' management plan and the communications management plan
  - Provide targeted messages to key stakeholders
- Obtain stakeholders' commitment
  - Call your stakeholders to action, involve them in project decisions throughout the project's life cycle
  - Communicate and obtain feedback
  - Make corrections and adjustments to the stakeholders' management strategy

You can't engage people with only empty words. The project manager has to be an example of the leadership he or she preaches.

Transparency in decisions and supporting evidence are also important to help in getting buy-in. Calling your audience to action is a very positive motivator, but you have to maintain engagement by giving feedback and open communications. The project manager has to create a sense of ownership and responsibility in key stakeholders, so that they are "personally" involved in the project.

The ability to influence people's thoughts and feelings, to generate their buy-in, has emerged as the paramount leadership skill (Walton, 2004). The strongest leaders are those who create a positive vision of the future, paint a big picture that generates action by tapping into people's emotions, ask for a commitment, and inspire their listeners to take steps toward the goal.

Remember, people want to be part of great achievements. Your project has to be good, and you have to show that to people so they want to support it. This is common sense uncommonly practiced. To do it, a great shift in the mindset is necessary.

Usually, project managers try to justify their projects using an internal point of view, forgetting that stakeholders' attention is focused on their own objectives and needs. The solution is to align the project's objectives to the stakeholders' expectations.

Imagine that you, as a project manager, have to present your project to a board of senior managers to get their approval and funding. Before that, you explain your project to the head of the PMO. Then you go to a meeting with senior managers.

You start something like, "Project XYZ is a front-end project to develop a satellite with powerful communications and controlling features. We need US$200 million and about 150 team members to accomplish this mission." The Board probably will question you about the benefits of your project, to which you answer within an internal project perspective also. Do you think you'd get the approval?

Another approach would be to convince and persuade the PMO with proper technical details of your project, emphasizing the strategic alignment and benefits it will provide. Now you have a supporter to be with you before the senior managers. You have to understand the motivation of the board, if you really want their support. Once you know what drives them, you can cast a vision that embraces their needs and worries.

Remember: We humans think in stories and images. A positive future is what all of us want to see. So, you have to develop a strategic story that "connects the dots" between the future the board wants and the project approval you want.

In Walton's (2004) words: "Strategic stories will provide you the key to the 'lock-box' of twenty-first-century buy-in: people's attention, emotions, and memories." Stakeholders' management is about access and impact using the four "ships:" partnership, sponsorship, leadership, and citizenship.

9.5 Complex Selling Approach

We've been talking a lot about the project manager acting as a seller. Sometimes people give bad connotations to the seller and selling. We are not talking about sellers of used cars trying to take advantage of other people.

Project managers have to create a strategic mindset that uses marketing and selling knowledge to build trust and create win-win situations. The focus is on finding similarities among stakeholders' expectations and casting a project vision that truly fulfills their needs. And this vision has to be effectively communicated to them.

To succeed, project managers have to strengthen their abilities related to the four "ships" of Chapter 4: partnership, sponsorship, leadership, and citizenship.

It is also important to think about authentic leadership, which creates a positive political environment through influence and persuasion, as we've seen in the previous topic. Cialdini (2000, quoted in Englund & Bucero, 2006) sums up the science and practice of persuasion like this: repay favors, behave consistently, follow the lead of similar others, favor the requests of those we like, and heed legitimate authorities and value scare resources.

The complex selling approach starts with stakeholders and environment assessment. The next step is to get buy-in, and involve and engage stakeholders, which implies lasting relationships in large intricate projects.

Environment Assessment

How is the project organized? How is the client's organization? Describe the organizational structure and political environment of the project. For example "The client organization has a weak project culture, and power is diffused. Functional managers are more important than project managers. The project organization is projectized and strongly results-oriented. There are also legal restrictions applied to the project concerning product safety."

Political Jungle

Remember the "animals" (Englund & Bucero, 2006) described in Chapter 7? It's time to give names to the animals! It's a fun, helpful way to assess stakeholders' power, influence, and impact.

Stakeholders' Roles

Here the objective is to understand the real role of stakeholders. Do they embrace their responsibilities? For example, "John U. is the sponsor, he is a busy executive and does not actively support projects."

Stakeholder Management Plan

- Establish a strategic storyline for your project
- Engage stakeholders
- Obtain stakeholders' commitment

Creating a proper project environment means that all players, especially sponsors, act with authenticity and integrity. People mean and believe what they say, and people do what they say, creating a trustworthy environment.

To create a sound stakeholder management plan, it is interesting to remember the SPIN Selling approach (Rackham, 1988):

- Situation—general information about the stakeholder and his or her environment
- Problem—worries and expectations of a stakeholder
- Implication—what will happen if the problem is not solved, consequences for the stakeholder
- Need of Payoff—how can I fix it and what benefits will this bring to stakeholders

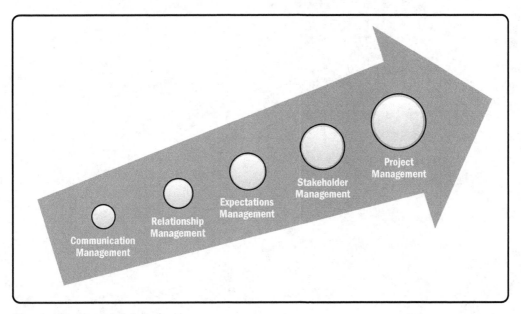

Figure 9-5: Successful projects.

Chapter 10

Keep in Touch!

The map is not the territory.

Alfred Korzybski

10.1 Stakeholder Management Along the Project Life Cycle

Approach organizational politics like a chess game; you have to be aware of the role and power of each chess piece. Sponsors and project managers need to think strategically to be able to influence people in organizations (Englund & Bucero, 2006, p. 188).

In project management, as in chess, success depends on your movements and the movements of your adversary. As a project manager, you don't have literally one adversary, but you have to deal with movements and expectations of a large number of conflicting stakeholders, meaning that it's more difficult to play project management than chess.

The chess game analogy is pretty interesting. Chess players learn and practice techniques; they study their opponents and create strategies to win. The project manager does the same. However, the trick is not only there. There is another key success factor: adaptability. Chess players change their strategies during a game to cope with their adversaries' movements. Stakeholder management strategies have to consider (Cleland, 1986):

- What resource allocations are required
- Why they are required
- When they are required
- Where they will be required
- How they will be used

Besides applying resources in a rational way, a good project manager has not only to be able to identify and understand stakeholders and to develop strategies to manage their expectations but also has to keep in touch, get feedback, and take preventive and corrective actions in stakeholder management. In managing either supportive or adverse project stakeholders by implementing stakeholder manage-ment strategies, we have to:

- Insure that stakeholders are involved to create a supporting coalition
- Provide a suitable security system to protect sensitive project information that might be used by adverse stakeholders to the detriment of the project
- Assess stakeholders as part of review meetings on an ongoing basis
- Maintain contact with stakeholders to get feedback, monitor stakeholder engagement and take corrective actions in stakeholder management
- Maintain periodical communications and provide information distribution properly

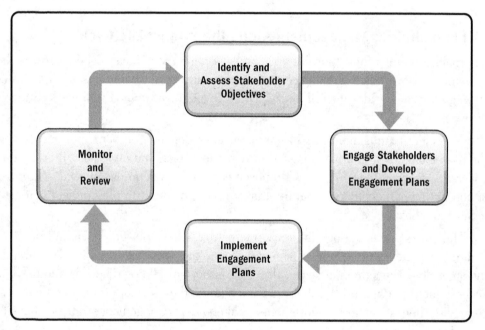

Figure 10-1: Stakeholder management life cycle.

Remember: Communication is not enough. Feedback is the breakfast of cham-pions, as Mersino (2007) stresses. The project manager has to monitor and control stakeholders' engagement. Project managers must pay attention to their project en-vironment. Too many projects threaten successful completion because of plenty of failure factors. However, most of them are intimately related to communication and stakeholders.

Invariably, requirements will change along the way. People's roles are going to change. Problems and challenges will emerge. And more. The best way to deal with all of this is building strong relationships.

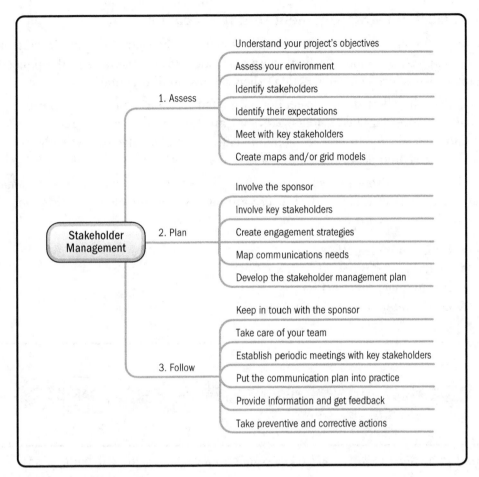

Figure 10-2: Stakeholder management.

We've seen that project success depends on stakeholders' satisfaction. But we've also seen that the stakeholders are not always right. Most of the time, they don't have proper knowledge about the project. This leads us to another important responsibility of project managers: putting up fences and boundaries. That is establishing objectives and positioning the project so that it can grow in the right direction.

We've seen that the project manager has to enforce his or her role as the project's source of information to prevent uncertainty and ambiguity. So be the first in line to get everyone's attention and commitment.

Positively, include a coalition of stakeholders that support you. Involve key stakeholders in decision making. Ask and answer questions about the potential to better accomplish the project's objectives. On the other hand, you have also to point out the negative consequences when projects lack stakeholders' support.

10.2 Stakeholder Management During Execution

It's in execution that we see if the project is going in the right direction. During the planning phases, it's more difficult for stakeholders to feel the taste of the project's results. Also, some stakeholders don't show interest until execution.

Part of the effort during execution is related to team management and part is focused on external stakeholders. Reviews are the proper place to get everyone's attention, collect feedback, get commitment, and restate the project's objectives. It's also the right time for replanning and realignment.

Depending on your project, you might have plenty of technical reviews. You may find other kinds of reviews also. There are four typical review types (Englund & Bucero, 2006):

- Initiation review (IR)
- Planning and proposal review (PPR)
- Procurement review (PR)
- Quality assurance review (QAR)

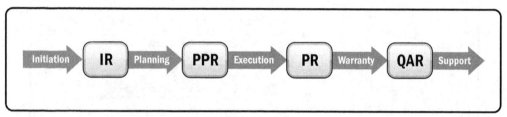

Figure 10-3: Typical project reviews (adapted from Englund & Bucero, 2006, p. 55)

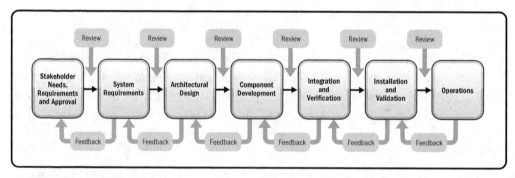

Figure 10-4: Stage-gate reviews.

The stage-gate reviews represented in Figure 10-3 are important to compliance and to decision making (Go/No Go).

You can have technical and managerial reviews all over the project. In the initiating and planning phases, technical reviews will be more common, while during execution it will be more common to have managerial reviews, monitoring and controlling meetings. Figure 10-4 shows technical reviews, according to the Defense Acquisition University; there are a lot of important reviews because it is related to very large and multifaceted projects and programs. The more large and multifaceted, the bigger the necessity for detailed control and checkpoints.

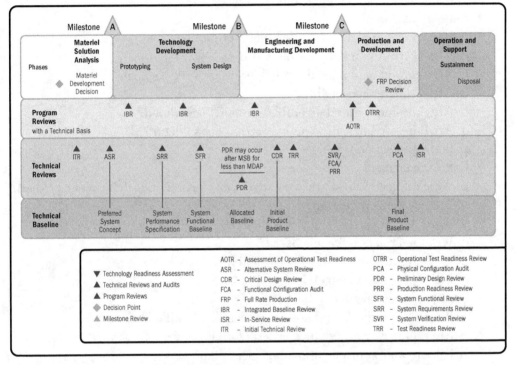

Figure 10-5: Technical reviews (Source: Defense Acquisition University, n.d.).

Communication will flow independent of reviews. You have to keep stakeholders informed periodically about the project. Milestones are of special interest to stakeholders, so you have to pay attention to them.

Another best practice is to use questionnaires to assess stakeholders' expectations. These questionnaires can be completed by the stakeholders, or you can do it yourself with the information you have, when stakeholders don't want or don't have time to do it. It's nice to have the project team answering these questionnaires also. When the answers of stakeholders differ a lot, then we have bad communication. If the project manager's answers are very different from the team and/or from key stakeholders, problems must be addressed.

Examples of proposed review questions, separated by knowledge area, are:

- Scope Management
  - Are requirements clearly and objectively stated?
  - Is the Scope Statement complete?

- Are all deliverables clearly defined?
- Is there a work breakdown structure (WBS)?
- Were requirements, deliverables, scope, and WBS accepted and validated by key stakeholders?
- Are there documented formal procedures for scope management, change management, and configuration management?
- Time Management
  - Is there a complete schedule? (not a preliminary one)
  - Is the schedule reflecting the WBS?
  - Are relevant activities identified for every work package?
  - Are estimates reasonable?
  - Are milestones and deliverables properly scheduled?
  - Are dependencies, especially external ones, identified?
  - Is the project on schedule?
- Cost Management
  - Were all needed resources estimated for the activities to be accomplished?
  - Is there a resource plan?
  - Were the procurement costs included?
  - Was the project risk considered?
  - Is the return on investment reasonable?
  - Is the project on budget?
- Quality Management
  - Were all standards and norms applicable identified?
  - Are there clear acceptance criteria for all deliverables?
  - Is there an improvement management plan?
  - Are there formal quality assurance and quality control procedures?
- Human Resources Management
  - Are roles and responsibilities clearly defined?
  - Is there an RACI matrix?
  - Is there a project organization chart?
  - Are team members' workloads acceptable?
  - Are there any over locations?
  - Are there formal procedures for rewards and appraisals?
- Communication Management
  - Are there regular meetings with proper stakeholders?
  - Is there a formal communication plan?
  - Is the information provided enough and on time?
- Risk Management
  - Was a risk identification conducted?
  - Were risks properly assessed?
  - Were risk responses planned?
  - Is there a formal risk management plan?

- Acquisition Management
  - o Is there a formal procurement plan?
  - o Is there a formal procedure for procurement?
  - o Is there legal support for contracts?
  - o Are suppliers and contractors satisfying expectations?
- Stakeholders Management
  - o Is the customer or client satisfied with the project?
  - o Is the sponsor involved in the project?
  - o Are key stakeholders engaged and committed?
  - o Are key stakeholders satisfied with project results and management?
  - o Is the project team happy and motivated?

This questionnaire can be used in the beginning of project execution. You can add more questions about project execution, related to monitoring and controlling, as necessary. Moreover, you can include indicators related to stakeholders' expectations and satisfaction along the way.

10.3 Back to Change Management

Although change management is more strictly related to scope management and integration, I had to mention it because stakeholders' are influenced by changes on the project.

In Chapter 3, we talked about change management processes and the Red Queen's Race, which means that users, clients, and stakeholders are never satisfied with features and requirements of a product or project. As time passes, they want to add more requirements and this leads to an ever-changing project and scope creep. Project managers have to say, "No." There is a time when we have to freeze requirements, a time to freeze specifications, architecture, and design, so that we can move on to construction.

Of course, you can change requirements along the way, but this has to follow a formal change management process. It has to become more difficult to make changes as time goes on.

And it's always necessary to assess impacts of change and pay special attention to configuration management. Here the steering committees or project boards come into play, which can have technical and business orientation. The purpose of the steering committee is to direct the project, not to manage it. The steering committee makes decisions that are beyond the project manager's authority. The ultimate goal is to ensure that each project continues to meet the needs of the organization and of the key stakeholders.

Here's what steering committee members need to do:

- Understand the strategic implications and outcomes of project outputs
- Have a broad understanding of project and business management issues

- Represent stakeholders' interests and help to balance conflicting interests
- Establish priorities and assign resources
- Ensure that project's outputs meet the requirements of the key stakeholders
- Foster positive communication between the project and other functional areas
- Review the status and progress of the project
- Make decisions beyond the project manager's authority

In practice, we have two types of committees in project management. The steering committee, as stated previously, is focused on business and organizational decisions regarding the project. We might also have a technical committee, sometimes called change control board (CCB), which focuses on technical aspects of the project and its scope.

It's very important that these two committees, if they are not the same, communicate effectively. It's the sponsor's role to manage these external project interfaces with the help of the project manager. A project management office may also help projects and committees to collaborate and be more effective.

One of the advantages of establishing a permanent project committee is that people get used to it; they share lessons learned, improving experience, and knowledge. Permanent committees enforce maturity in project management.

10.4 Monitoring and Controlling

You get what you measure. If you don't measure, people won't do it. If you don't understand what you're measuring, how would you know if you're on the right way?

These questions are crucial to project management. Once somebody asked me if I could summarize project management into one word and I said "Control." It is simplistic, but it gets the idea.

Why do we use best practices, methodologies, tools, and techniques in project management? Because we want to achieve consistent and repetitive success in projects, right? And how do we do that? By properly identifying needs, planning the project, executing it and taking corrective actions along the way. This is Plan-Do-Check-Act.

You can only control what you've completely defined. All measures and project indicators are derived from the project planning. That's why control summarizes, in some way, project management. It's not possible to control if I didn't complete planning or if I'm not executing.

Proactivity, one of the most important characteristics of a project manager, is very important in monitoring and controlling. Don't stay behind your desk waiting for people to come up with issues, they probably won't tell you the bad news. You need to know everything, or almost everything, about your project to take actions.

And as long as you have the right information, you can communicate it to your stakeholders and improve these relationships to get support. A stakeholder would probably feel betrayed when a project manager brings a big problem that has been going on for the last four months.

Monitoring and controlling has to be a habit. Using lag indicators, we can have an idea of what happened on that project and take corrective actions; we can also obtain valuable lessons learned. Using lead indicators and project data, it's possible to forecast trends and take preventive actions based on scenario planning, for example.

Jurgen Appelo (2010) mentions the Conant-Ashby Theorem. Appelo said delegation of control is the best way to keep projects manageable. The theorem states that "Every good regulator of a system must have a model of that system."

In other words, to control, we have to plan (or model) something. Project management is about divide and conquer, breaking the project into small work packages so that you can manage it. And here we have another problem: the control of a system can only be as good as the quality of the information available from the system. The less information there is about a system, or the less accurate it is, the worse our ability to plan, model, or control it.

10.5 Project Management Metrics

Strictly related to monitoring and controlling are the project management metrics, key performance indicators (KPIs), and dashboards. We use the project data collected to make decisions and to inform stakeholders. It's obvious that we have to transform that data in valuable information by organizing it.

Harold Kerzner (2011) says that stakeholders are getting more sophisticated. Before, stakeholders' involvement in projects was more passive than active, meaning stakeholders were not engaged and involved in project decisions. They were not worried about how the project would be conducted; their focus was mainly on the deliverables at the end of the project.

With more involved projects and sophisticated stakeholders, the situation now is very different. Stakeholders are not only results oriented but they also want to influence the processes and phases of the project. Stakeholders are not passively waiting for the project manager to bring them the information he or she thinks is relevant; stakeholders now demand actively that the project manager provide the information they want.

This is a new paradigm that project managers face. As stakeholder involvement becomes more active than passive, project managers must change the way they used to do stakeholder management.

We already know that project managers have to work closely with all of the stakeholders to understand the requirements of the project, they have to involve and engage stakeholders in decision making and get their buy-in and commitment. However, this new paradigm of sophisticated stakeholders created new information and communication demands.

It's not only to identify communication needs of stakeholders (Who – What – When – How) but also to discuss and develop metrics to monitor the project's objectives and stakeholders' expectations. It's impossible to manage all this information without using an information system to provide automatic and real time status reports, preferably in dashboard formats. Kerzner (2011) enumerates some commonly used stakeholder metrics:

- Percentage of work packages adhering to the schedule;
- Percentage of work packages adhering to the budget;
- Number of assigned resources versus planned resources;
- Percentage of actual versus planned baselines completed to date;
- Percentage of actual versus planned best practices used;
- Project complexity factor;
- Customer satisfaction ratings;
- Number of critical assumptions made;
- Percentage of critical assumptions that have changed;
- Number of cost revisions;
- Number of schedule revisions;
- Number of scope change review meetings;
- Number of critical constraints;
- Percentage of work packages with a critical risk designation; and
- Net operating margins.

We are not going to dig into key performance indicators or dashboards. A complete reference is *Project Management Metrics, KPIs, and Dashboards: A Guide to Measuring and Monitoring Project Performance* by Harold Kerzner (2011).

The idea you have to get from here is that stakeholders are becoming more knowledgeable in project management. Project managers have to learn better ways of providing timely information to stakeholders beyond Microsoft Project reports.

10.6 Changing Expectations, Not Specifications

This is a topic that I want to enforce. Expectations are influenced by the complex selling approach, and project managers need to know how to negotiate and persuade.

Back to systems engineering, there is a time when we have to freeze requirements. Then there is a time when we have to freeze the scope, design, and so on— until we get to the construction and implementation phases.

Although it's kind of obvious that changes cost more as time passes, many stakeholders don't grasp this. Project managers have to reinforce the importance of proper requirements and scope definition to build a solid project management plan. The trick to manage stakeholders' expectations is to set objectives clearly and establish indicators agreed on. A good business case document, being updated during the project, helps managing expectations and avoiding unnecessary changes.

The stage boundaries in PRINCE2™ provide opportunities to review both technical aspects and business justification of a project, ensuring that everybody is on the same page.

Chapter 11

Team Management

Never discourage anyone who continually makes progress, no matter how slow.

Plato

11.1 Your Closest Stakeholders

Who are your closest stakeholders? Well, the client may be nagging you frequently; your sponsor may want weekly reports or meetings, but your project team will probably be around you all the time. One of the consequences is that you can't fake leadership. They will see you every day; they will watch your behavior, and they will dance according to the music. If you act loosely, if you don't make people accountable, they will understand the message and behave accordingly.

You might be saying now "Is my team the closest stakeholders I have? My team is 1,000 people, and I meet with only 15 of them daily . . . I don't even know some of the other team members." You have a point with that. In large intricate projects, project managers can't meet regularly with all the team members because there are a lot of them, maybe even located in different places around the world. No problem. You'll be a leader of leaders.

Delegation of control creates management scalability. You push decisions and responsibilities down to a level where someone has information that is smaller and more accurate. The project manager will count on his or her project management team, or core team, to help him or her manage downwards. Your management team members have to be accountable for their decisions. They need responsibilities and authority to carry on their tasks. Here leadership plays a crucial role: project managers, as leaders, set direction, motivate, and create boundaries to their core team. This "culture" will propagate through management team members to the rest of the team. Don't forget that you get what you measure. So, if you don't make your core team accountable, they probably won't make their subordinates accountable.

We can say that the role of a leader is to create a chain of leadership. Management is strictly related to leadership as we have to plan, organize and control, not only inspire. Appelo (2010) stated, "Smart managers understand that they must try to make as few decisions as possible. The decisions should be made for people who have the proper accurate information in lower levels."

For example, suppose you are the CEO of Apple, occupying the position of the legendary Steve Jobs. Would you make decisions about how to organize equipment inside a plant in China? Would you make decisions about how to develop a smarter touch screen technology? No, you shouldn't. What the CEO does is set direction and empower people below him or her to make the right decisions. Maybe the CEO is more like a chief evangelist officer than a chief executive officer.

Another advantage of building a leadership chain is that governance is naturally enforced because it is spread all over the project organization. Communication flows fearlessly and improvements are fueled by people's suggestions and ideas.

11.2 Human Resource Planning

The identification of stakeholders must go beyond the internal stakeholders, which are, in general, supportive of project strategies since they are an integral part of the project team (Cleland, 1986). However, the project manager should not forget to insure that these internal stakeholders play an important and supportive role. Such a supportive role is usually forthcoming since the project manager has some degree of authority and influence over these individuals.

Human resource planning is a progressive process. In project planning phases, there are many iterations. The more detail becomes available, the more detailed we can plan.

While defining scope and activities, we start to get a better idea of resources needed. The problem is that many project managers think that scope-time-cost is all that we need to manage a project. Human resources focuses only on answering "who does what when" or the RACI matrix.

However, HR management is much more than that. We have not only to identify people needed but also be specific about the knowledge and experience of them. The HR plan includes also appraisals, training, personal improvement, and team building.

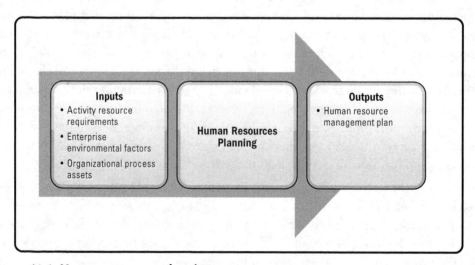

Figure 11-1: Human resources planning.

The main inputs are the activity resource requirements that derive from scope definition and activities definition. And the main output is the HR Plan, which includes:

- HR requirements,
- Roles and responsibilities,
- Organizational chart, and
- Staffing management plan.

The HR plan, in its staffing management plan, defines how people will be managed. An important human resource function is to create recognition and rewards systems, and those systems are a required part of the HR management plan. Another important function is to improve the team members' competencies, which is a responsibility of the project manager.

Projects are not only to deliver products or end results; they are great opportunities for professional and personal development. The project manager has to care about that because there will be new projects in the future, and the organization will benefit from better professionals and high-performance teams created in previous projects.

Although most of HR management is done in the executing process group, planning HR management must not be overlooked. It's a big error trying to manage HR "on demand" in project execution without a plan. It is interesting that one of the tools and techniques is "networking." Why? Because the project manager has to negotiate to obtain human resources. Sometimes he even has to convince people to work on his project.

The project manager must continually confirm resource availability, never take it for granted. Another cause of failure in projects is that project managers think the plan is the territory. That is, the plan is reality. In HR management, it's common not to get exactly the resources you asked for and you have to assess the risks and impacts on your project.

Imagine that your project was estimated based upon Grade 5 employees being assigned. In the execution phase, you get Grade 3 employees (i.e., Grade 3 is less qualified than a Grade 5). This could be a strong indication that you are heading for a schedule slippage. Every organization has employees' levels and they reflect knowledge, experience, qualification, and other aspects that are extremely important in project planning.

The project manager has to properly specify what skills and experience human resources must have to work on the project. That's why position description and detailed human resources needs are important. It's clearly obvious that we need a plan, formal activities and documentation in human resources management.

All training and team-building activities have to be formally planned and are a required part of the RH management plan. The project manager must also track team member performance, do appraisals, and maybe inform the HR department.

There are two very useful tools because of HR planning:

- Organizational chart (or organizational breakdown structure)
  - This chart demonstrates how your human resources are organized, structured, and managed. It shows the hierarchical relationships, reporting structure and more.
- Responsibility Assignment Matrix (RAM)
  - The RAM matrix demonstrates roles and responsibilities, indicating who is involved in what task and what that person will have to do. This is also known as the RACI matrix (Responsible, Accountable, Consulted and Informed)

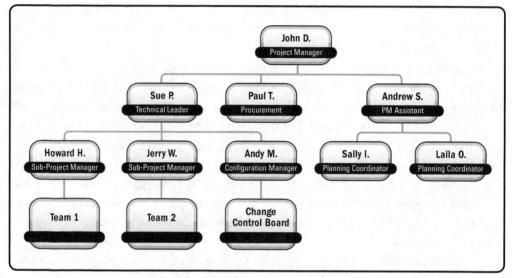

Figure 11-2: Project organizational chart.

Table 11-1 RACI matrix.

	Planning	Subproject 1	Subproject 2
John D.	R, A	I	I
Sue P.	R	R, A	R, A
Paul T.	C	I	I
Andrew S.	R, A	C, I	C, I

R = Responsible , A = Accountable , I = Inform , C = Consult

Both the organizational chart and the RACI matrix should be better detailed.

The project manager uses organizational process assets to derive HR politics and procedures to the project. In the end, the HR plan defines:

- HR needs qualitatively and quantitatively;
- Training needs;

- Labor and safety requirements;
- HR allocation by tasks;
- Rewards and recognition system;
- How people will be assigned to the project;
- Performance appraisals; and
- Disciplinary rules.

Although the HR plan is a cornerstone to project success, the real proof of fire is to put it into practice. To deal with people is never an easy task.

11.3 Motivational Theories

Human resource responsibilities increase as the size of the project team increases. The complexity of the project and qualification of team members required add extra work in RH management.

Before we study team building, it's essential to take a look at some motivational theories. Interpersonal skills are extremely important, as you already know. Since Daniel Goleman and Dale Carnegie, emotional intelligence (EI) has been well recognized.

Emotional intelligence embraces social abilities, political intelligence, and communication skills. Mastering soft skills is not easy but at least we can understand what it takes to motivate others. The oldest theory, I think, is Maslow's Hierarchy of Needs.

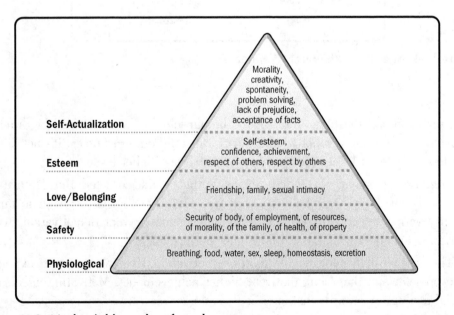

Figure 11-3: Maslow's hierarchy of needs.

Figure 11-3 represents the original Maslow pyramid. There are five levels of human necessities. Interestingly, Maslow says people don't care about higher levels if lower levels are not satisfied; if physiological or safety needs are not satisfied, why would somebody look for self-actualization? In a way, Maslow's theory is too focused on materialism. We understand that a hungry student won't perform well most of the time. But there are deep strong emotions and feelings that push people beyond their physiological, safety, or any other needs toward a master goal, generally related to esteem and self-actualization.

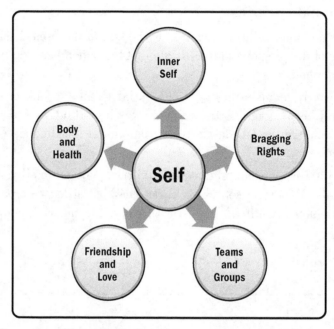

Figure 11-4: Alternative "hierarchy" of needs.

I prefer to use a circle of interrelated human needs. We are driven by different motivators, and our motivation changes with time and circumstances. It's not necessary to satisfy lower level requirements to care about higher levels.

Frederick Herzberg extended Maslow's theory and created the Motivation-Hygiene Theory. His theory holds there are two factors you strive for: hygiene agents and motivating agents. In summary, hygiene agents prevent demotivation, while motivating agents provide stimuli for higher performance.

The absence of hygiene agents creates demotivation. Hygiene agents are expected to be present, and they don't motivate higher achievements. Motivating agents are special feelings or rewards that energize people.

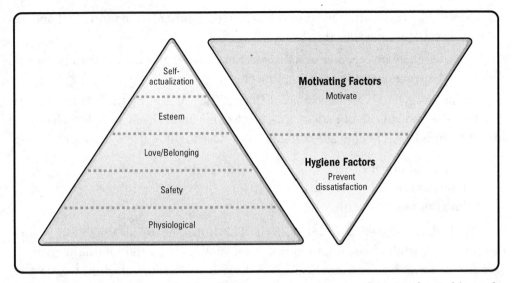

Figure 11-5: Herzberg's motivation-hygiene theory compared to Maslow's hierarchy of needs.

Another well-known theory is Douglas McGregor's Theory X and Y. McGregory believed that there are two types of employees:

- X employees are lazy, don't like to work and have to be micromanaged to get them to do any of their responsibilities.
- Y employees are motivated, self-led, and responsible, they want to do their assignments and need low supervision.

There are many theories about motivation and it is impossible to define rules that apply to everyone. We need a contingent approach to deal with different people, different expectations, and different circumstances. Emotional and social intelligences are competitive advantages nowadays.

I also like to think about the positive reinforcement. Karen Pryor (2006) mentions research showing that following a behavior with a pleasant consequence increases the behavior. Both are true and obvious, in a way. However, in practice we don't apply it.

Karen Pryor says that we usually use the laws of positive reinforcement inappropriately, which produces bad results. She emphasizes that positive reinforcement is not a system of reward and punishment. Reinforcement is an event that occurs during or upon completion of a behavior and increases the likelihood of that behavior occurring in the future.

Reinforcers is feedback tailored to people and situations. You can use them to increase the likelihood of good behaviors and to change or correct behaviors that are not desired. The trick is that the payoff has to make sense to each individual and has to be presented on time with the desired behavior.

If you want a team member to deliver better reports, give him or her reinforcers, which can be a simple praise or compliment.

On the other hand, we have Daniel Pink (2011) defending that we have a new driving force beyond the old stick-and-carrot motivators. Because of the change in the type of work that people are doing, he says that we have three drives:

- Biological drive,
- Punishment and reward drive, and
- Inner or internal drive.

The first two drivers are well known. The third one is, as Pink (2011) says, the surprising truth about what motivates us. Motivated by the internal driver, we accomplish tasks because they are interesting, because they are fun, because we like them, because they contribute.

Pink (2011) states that if-then rewards are only good for simple, straightforward, rule-based tasks or behavior, which are strictly related to the industrialized world.

Now that we have knowledge workers (Drucker, 1999), motivation changed. For non-routine, conceptual work, stick-and-carrot motivators don't work so well. The third drive proposed by Pink (2011) expands our understanding of self-actualization; it pushes motivation to the bragging rights that I've mentioned previously.

Highly educated people carrying on complex, creative, and conceptual work, defined as knowledge workers, are more motivated by the third driver, something about mastery, purpose, and contributing, than biological and if-then rewards motivators. Here comes to mind a great piece of advice from Dale Carnegie (2009) that we should give the other person a fine reputation to live up to and see what happens. It seems that Carnegie knew, in the 1930s, the surprising truth about what motivates us, proved by Daniel Pink.

What motivates us is a mix of challenge and self-knowledge, which is intrinsic related to self-actualization. Great challenges impose anxiety and even fear in people who don't have the necessary knowledge. On the other hand, the absence of challenge demotivates people with high-level skills.

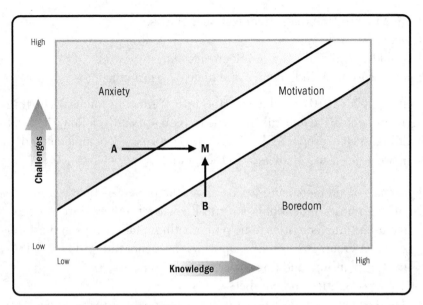

Figure 11-6: The motivation channel.

Project managers have to pay attention so that team members stay, most of the time, in the motivation channel. High skilled team members have to be moved from point B to M by increasing challenge, which can be done by assigning them to complex work, delegating and giving them responsibilities over tasks. Less skilled team members have to be moved from point A to M by being assigned to tasks compatible with their knowledge and skills.

11.4 Team Building

Now that we've refreshed some concepts and theories on motivation, we can think of team building in a different way. Usually we believe that building a team is only a matter of creating purpose and respect. However, it is more than that if we think that these people will probably have to work together in the future. They may also be asked to give more than their best in favor of the team. So, we can think of teams as a kind of family, and this requires growing relationships.

When you have a dozen people that have worked together before, it's pretty easy. You just need to assign roles and everything will be okay. However, dealing with a large group of people that never worked together before is more complicated. We've seen that it takes time and effort to plan human resources requirements, staffing management and RH improvement:

- Identify people you need;
- Create detailed description of positions;
- Plan how you'll use people in the project, roles and responsibilities;

- Define hierarchy, create organizational charts;
- Create a rewards system;
- Plan individual and team development; and
- Plan how to track individual's and team's performance.

Jurgen Appelo (2010) emphasizes the term "growing teams." He thinks that building teams doesn't catch the real idea. Teams usually follow the well-known team building stages proposed by Tuckman (1965) and complemented by other authors, as we've seen in Chapter 2. To recapitulate:

- Forming—team meets and learns about the project's objectives
  - o In this phase, individuals start to know each other. Here we can develop team-building activities to help in creating relationships and establishing a sense of group. We can also apply assessments like MBTI or DISC to help in staff planning and future performance reports.
- Storming—politics and conflicts
  - o The second stage is when the team members already know each other, which means there is a political environment being established. The initial motivation goes back to reality, and there may be conflicts over many issues from tasks and responsibilities to more complicated subjects. It is time to reinforce trust and respect. It is also a time to establish ground rules.
- Norming—team members adjust their behavior to the team
  - o At some point, team members develop work habits that make teamwork more natural and fluid. Energy and motivation increases from the lower levels of the storming stage.
- Performing—synergy and efficiency
  - o Although it seems every team passes through the same Tuckman's stage, it is not like that. Few teams achieve the performing stage, which is like a flow state. In this stage, there are few conflicts, the team is more self-managed and needs little supervision. It is an environment of collaboration where the job gets done smoothly and effectively in higher standards.
- Adjourning—closure and departing
  - o Every project has an end. In this stage, people may feel vulnerable and worried about their futures. The project manager's job should help in this transition where people need to be relocated in the organization. Of course, it's a time to review, document lessons learned, recognize the work done, and celebrate the end of the project.

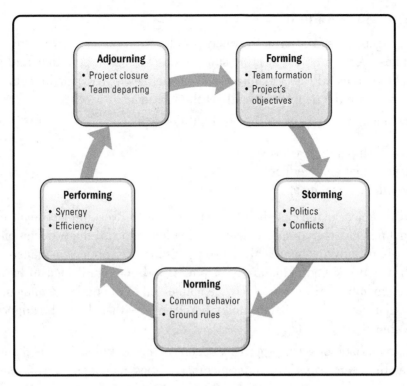

Figure 11-7: Team building stages (Adapted from Tuckman, 1965).

A common misunderstanding is that a team won't get back to a lower stage once it gets to a higher one. Even if your team is in the norming or in the performing stages, it can go back to the storming stage. Consequently, it's important to monitor team behavior and expectations. Besides, if you change more than 30% of your team, you'd probably have to go back to the forming stage and carry on team building activities again.

An effective way to drive the project team through these team-building stages is to involve them in decisions. To be able do that, team members need to understand the high-level methodology process within the context of the project. That is, they need to see the big picture shown by the project manager.

The project manager has to assure that everyone knows the project's objective. Individuals have also to be able to identify phases, major activities, and deliverables to commit to the project and to the team.

The project manager has to be someone respected in the organization and needs not only project management experience but also some technical knowledge and business context knowledge. Team members must recognize the project manager as their leader.

11.5 Team Management

Team management starts formally when people are assigned to the project. This startup phase, known as the forming stage is crucial, setting the tone and pace for the rest of the project. Project managers have to actively participate in team building because these are the people that will get the job done.

In team management, we will focus on three aspects:

- Leadership and motivation
- Assessment and feedback
- Conflict management

Ideally, project managers should spend time with every project team member, ironing out misunderstandings, miscommunication, and varying expectations. However, this is usually not practical or even possible. So, project managers have to establish a network and a hierarchy of power and communication to assure that every team member will, in some way, be connected to the project manager. Project managers delegate to levels below him or her, decisions that should be aligned to the project's objectives.

A characteristic of great project managers is that they listen to as many stakeholders as they can, especially team members. Good managers clarify reasons for their priorities, which motivates and involves stakeholders.

In team management, project managers also have to rely on technology. Teleconferences and videoconferences are efficient ways to communicate and share information with distributed teams, saving a lot of time.

11.5.1 Leadership and Motivation

We've already seen motivation theories previously. These theories provide the basis for managers to act as leaders. Project managers have to know what motivates people and how to act to provide and enhance motivation, which leads us to the leadership styles.

Table 11-2: Leadership styles according to Mersino (2007, p. 217).

Leadership Style	EI Competencies	When to Apply	Traps/When not to Apply
Visionary	• Inspirational Leadership • Self-Confidence • Self-Awareness • Empathy	• Apply as often as possible, in particular when project manager wants to inspire team to grow and be creative.	• When team members are more senior or have unique expertise and project manager's vision-casting will sound hollow.
Coaching	• Developing Others • Self Awareness • Empathy	• When team members trust and want the leader to invest in them. • When developing people is important.	• Team may lose sight of project goals in effort to develop people.
Affiliative	• Relationship Management • Empathy • Conflict Management	• When it is important to bring team together or when healing team divisions is necessary.	• Some affiliative leaders fall prey to being liked by others or lose sight of the project goals and objectives.
Democratic	• Teamwork and Collaboration • Conflict Management • Influence	• When the leader needs to get the input from the team to make decisions; to reach consensus.	• Leader must be open to input from the team. • Team must have valuable input to offer. • Team members may find leader indecisive or bogged down in endless meetings.
Pacesetting	• Achievement • Initiative	• Works well when used with either the visionary or affiliative styles, or when leader applies empathy and self-management to counter the pressure placed on the team. • Works to get the best performance from an experienced and competent team.	• Pacesetters often lack empathy, self-awareness; communication skills, and emotional self management; may communicate that goals are more important than people. • Team members may feel anxious, criticized, and unappreciated.
Commanding	• Influence • Achievement • Initiative	• Emergencies, crisis, or turnaround projects. • When leader is significantly more experienced than the team.	• Use only in those situations where appropriate and balance with other styles.

Mersino (2007) brings us a very good summary of leadership styles, which I reproduced here. He gives us clues on advantages and disadvantages of each style and he suggests when to apply them. For more information, I advise you to read his book, where he explains these styles with more details and there are a lot of other interesting topics there.

Besides Mersino (2007), there are many theories in leadership. Without the discovery of a leadership gene, we can learn and master leadership behavior. Another good reference in project management leadership is Jack Ferraro's (2008) *The Strategic Project Leader.*

A project manager who aspires to be a leader needs to discover his or her stakeholders' (or followers') preferences. Although the project manager usually has the formal authority and power over the project; it is common for stakeholders to challenge the project manager's role as a leader, creating tacit and explicit conflicts that should be addressed by the project manager. This said, it is easy to understand that knowing different leadership styles and theories and when to apply them, is useful.

- Situational leadership—The project environment impacts leadership results, making it necessary to adopt different behaviors and to use different skills when circumstances change. There is a best behavior (best practices in leadership) for every situation and the leader can apply it.

- Contingent leadership—Considers not only the situational leadership (stakeholders' characteristics and project environment) but also the personal style of the project manager as a leader. This theory says that it's almost impossible for a leader to mimic every best behavior in a variety of complex situations. In a way, it is derived from the situational leadership.
- Transactional leadership—There is a contractual relationship between the leader and follower, where the follower agrees to get the job done in exchange for a reward, typically financial. The transactional leader simply distributes work to the team members and holds them accountable for getting the job done.
- Transformational leadership—Transformational leadership goes beyond situational and contingency leadership styles to focus on individuals and on their personal development. It seems to be better adapted to knowledge workers because it strengthens purpose and contributing feelings.

The situational and transformational leadership theories are more people-oriented while the transactional leadership is more task oriented. The first creates and fosters a collaborative and participative environment, while the second is usually authoritative and strictly results oriented. Despite the supportive approach of transformational leadership, sometimes this is not the best style because it is not easy to put it into practice.

The situational leadership allies inspiration to detailed action tailored according to circumstances, and this is where its power resides: being adaptive as a situational leader while still maintaining focus on the job to be done. As a drawback, transformational leadership can become vague and ambiguous, resulting in unachievable dreams. Transformational leadership is better indicated in mentoring and coaching knowledge workers, preparing young talents to higher organizational positions and creating new leaders.

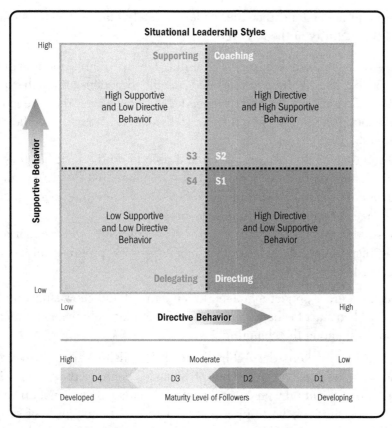

Figure 11-8: Situational leadership theory (Hersey & Blanchard, 1977).

In situational leadership theory (Situational leadership theory, n.d.), there are four basic leadership styles:

- S1: Telling—It is the most directive style, characterized by one-way communication in which the leader defines roles of individuals and details how the work should be done.
- S2: Selling—The leader is still providing directive, but he is also supportive, using a two-way communication approach, listening to followers and persuading them.
- S3: Participating—The leader is very supportive, trying to develop followers through shared decision making and strengthening trust in relationships with individuals.
- S4: Delegating—The leader is still involved in monitoring the team's progress and to help when needed; however, decisions and responsibility have been passed to individuals.

It is easy to understand that the leadership style that best fits a situation will depend on the maturity of the followers:

- M1—Individuals lack the specific skills, they are unable and unwilling to accomplish the tasks. Individuals need specific directions and high supervision.
- M2—Individuals may still lack specific skills; however, they are more proactive and willing to get the job done. Individuals still need specific directions but not high supervision.
- M3—Individuals are experienced and able to do the task but they lack the confidence to take on responsibility. It is common that they are young talents. Individuals don't need specific directions, they know how to get the job done. They need support, advice, and encouragement.
- M4—individuals are experienced, self-confident, and comfortable with their responsibilities. The leader monitors work progress and strengthens relationships.

To become a great project manager, know yourself and show sincere interest for other people. Then start to shape your behavior; act like a chameleon, quickly interpreting and acting upon the changing

Appelo (2010) explains the Ashby's Law of Requisite Variety, which says that the person with the greatest flexibility of behavior controls the system. However, remember all that I said previously. Stakeholders' management is not about manipulation, it is about finding the tipping point where a virtuous circle of support and collaboration results in effectiveness toward project results.

11.5.2 Conflicts Management

Invariably, the project manager will be involved in team conflicts. If there are people, there are conflicts.

Invest time in team building activities because the stages proposed by Tuckman (1965) need time to be completed. It may seem that your team suddenly jumped suddenly from the forming to the norming or to the performing stages. This is unreal. Probably, there are hidden politics and unsolved conflicts that will throw your project into a hurricane of conflicts (back to the storming stage) when you most need cooperation and collaboration. And you'll regret a lot.

The project manager is responsible for setting team boundaries and supporting the creation of ground rules. Respect, transparency, and trust are crucial to succeed in intricate projects because of interactions and dependencies.

Project managers have to listen to many team members, even when the messages conveyed are not easy to receive (Englund & Bucero, 2006). When people feel valued, they are motivated to contribute more.

Happy team members work better; they cooperate better, and they collaborate better. Consequently, performance improves, coaching and mentoring between senior and junior team members happen smoothly; conflicts usually are solved among team members themselves. With multicultural team members, the project manager has to be prepared to deal with different cultures and values. Integrating international team members has to be done carefully, because lack of cultural sensitivity distracts them from the tasks and may even cause bigger issues.

Every conflict should be addressed as soon as it arises. First, team members involved in the conflict have to try to solve it. To do that, there has to be open communications and trust; team building is critical.

If team members involved can't find a solution or reach an agreement, it is time to escalate the problem, which can be done through a coach, a mediator, or even with the help of other team members. Ground rules should be clear and easy to understand and the problem has to be analyzed objectively.

Even with third parties intervention, if the conflict is not resolved, it is time for the project manager to intervene. It is not that the project manager didn't do anything before, he was not watching. The project manager is responsible for the project team as a whole and has always to help and support team members. However, it is important to develop a sense of responsibility and commitment in the project team, giving them authority and independence to make some decisions and to solve issues.

The project manager delegates conflict management to the team in an attempt to improve maturity. On the other hand, if a particular conflict is getting out of control, the project manager should take action. The project manager can try conciliation or take administrative and disciplinary action. If the project manager cannot solve the conflict, he or she doesn't have enough power or authority; he or she addresses the problem with the sponsor or the HR department and so on, until the conflict is resolved. These are some ways of resolving conflicts:

- Forcing
  - One person, who has power and authority, forces a solution, despite the opinions of others. Although this may seem to be a permanent solution, there can be other conflicts due to demotivation, lack of cooperation, and even resistance. This is a win-lose resolution, where people have to accept what is imposed by someone else. A classic example is when the boss says, "Do it because I'm telling you to do." It is somewhat obvious that this is not the best resolution, but sometimes it is necessary that the project manager play this boss role. When dealing with team members with low maturity levels (remember situational leadership?), you'll probably have to force some decisions.

- Smoothing or Accommodating
  - o It is a temporary way of forgetting that there is a problem. Sometimes, this approach emphasizes the areas of agreement or tries to make conflicts seem less important. When a compromise is reached, maybe not everybody is happy, but the majority is less unhappy than when you use forcing. On the other hand, because it does not lead to a permanent solution, the conflict may become bigger due to not dealing with it properly in time.
- Compromise
  - o Compromise is different from smoothing because it faces the conflict and deals with it. People involved in the conflict negotiate and agree in giving and taking to reach a solution. If this is an open and clear process, and if there is commitment to the solution, it will lead to a win-win permanent situation.
- Confrontation or problem solving
  - o As the name says, it is the best way to solve problems or conflicts. Confrontation is an objective and fact-based approach to solving conflicts. People involved in the conflict expose their issues and uncover the underlying facts, then they try to find the best solution together. Notice that it is not a give and take negotiation; it is a collaborative work to solve a problem that may affect the project, whose objectives are placed higher than personal objectives.
- Withdrawal or avoidance
  - o Avoidance is not properly a conflict resolution approach. The conflict is not solved and maybe neither discussed. One of the parties leaves and refuses to discuss the conflict. As a result, the conflict is not solved and relationship is damaged. Some say that this is the worst conflict resolution technique.

The role of the project manager is to defend the objectives of the project but also to build and keep relationships with stakeholders by managing their expectations, involving, and engaging them. Damaging a relationship with stakeholders is usually bad because it hurts the project environment. A sour attitude is contagious, it promotes competitive individualism and enhances resistance.

Therefore, the first step is always to assure that there is really a problem, and that it is not just a matter of bad communication or misunderstanding. Then you can try one of the resolutions of conflicts approach.

It is wise to keep an issue log, so you can keep track of conflicts, particularly inside your team, throughout the project. You should try also to prevent conflicts by enforcing team building and ground rules, and making objectives, roles and responsibilities clear to everyone.

11.5.3 Feedback

Performance reports are part of life. The project manager may be responsible for providing performance reports on team members, especially when it is a long project with full-time assignments. Feedback and performance reports are also parts of team building activities because they stimulate open communications and enhance trust.

Remember that the proper development of the team is critical to the success of the project? The project manager, as a leader and manager, will show in practice his or her values and enforce ground rules, or not, when he is in contact with team members. Feedback is a powerful tool to motivate and engage people because they feel respected and valuable; they feel that they are important and that they can improve themselves.

Giving feedback should not be only criticism. Actually, feedback has to be a reinforcement of good habits and performance as well as an opportunity to correct poor or bad behavior.

Project managers have to show interest in their team members, which is only possible if they are interested in them for real. As long as project managers really care about their teams, they can identify opportunities of improvement and suggest feedback. Feedback has to be objective and to direct or propose ways of improvement that may be discussed with the team member.

If I criticize your job in a general way, let's say "Dear reader, you are doing it all wrong! Why are you reading this page and not the next one? Haven't you finished the book? You're late! And I don't really think that you are understanding . . ."

Awful, isn't it? Sorry for that, it was just an example. This type of criticism, I don't even know if we can call it feedback, is the worst you can do. The other person won't know what he has to do to improve; there was no objectivity. It was useless. Worse, it hurts the listener, and puts him or her in a defensive approach. And he or she would probably get angry or sad. It would be very different if I said: "Dear reader, I'm seeing that you are a little sleepy. Are you paying attention? Do you think it would be better if you take a look at the beginning of the chapter to recap? Or maybe you could read it tomorrow, if you prefer."

As I said, feedback is not always negative. You should point out accomplishments and praise team members because this is a strong motivator. It is important to recognize who is doing a great job; it will state higher standards and show team members that you are paying attention to their contributions. These are some tools and techniques related to feedback.

- Observation and conversation
  - Being near all your team members might not be possible, but the benefits are worth it. It's difficult to understand team members' feelings and points of view if you're communicating through someone else. Besides, once your team perceives you as available and willing to listen, they will bring all their issues, related to the project or not, as soon as they arise, which is very good.

- Project performance appraisals
  - o Performance appraisals are periodical evaluations of team members' individual performance and of the team's performance as a whole. It is a great opportunity to identify training needs and issues, to clarify roles and responsibilities, and to set goals for the future.

In very big project teams, it is not possible for the project manager to keep in touch with all team members. Considering that the project manager acts as a leader, he or she should direct the behavior of followers by his or her attitude and example, establishing a hierarchical chain of trust and openness where these previous tools and techniques are employed in every level.

No matter what type of appraisal is conducted, project managers are responsible for and should contribute to the performance appraisals of the project team members.

Chapter 12

Conclusions

Man's mind, once stretched by a new idea,
never regains its original dimensions.

Oliver Wendell Holmes

12.1 The Epic Challenge of Managing Stakeholders

Dear reader, thank you for your patience. I hope that this book was useful and helpful. We are now going to recap some important aspects of stakeholder and communications management. We will also introduce some other topics in stakeholder management, knowledge management, and leadership.

A central premise underlying the concept of project stakeholder management is that the project manager should make deliberate attempts to exert influence on project stakeholders so that they deliver their contributions to the project (Jepsen & Eskerod, 2008). In contrast, another central premise is that project managers have limited resources and should allocate these resources in such a way that they achieve the best possible results.

The law of diminishing returns is the decrease in the marginal output of a production process as the amount of a single factor of production is increased, while the amounts of all other factors of production stay constant. As an analogy, in project management, increasing efforts in stakeholder management will bring diminishing benefits to the success of a project.

If the marginal gains reduce as the amount of resources is increased, efforts are better expended and spread across a range of stakeholders than concentrated on a few, because initial efforts yield a higher benefit than will later efforts. This entails that the stakeholder analysis should uncover how necessary the prospective contribution or involvement from each stakeholder is for the project, as well as the power of the stakeholders and the possibility to influence them (Jepsen & Eskerod, 2008).

12.2 Over-communication Is Never a Problem

Communication is pointed out as the single biggest problem, the root of many other causes of failure in project management. And this is not our privilege, it is also true for many other management endeavors.

This implies every effort in communicating abundantly and clearly is worthwhile. Listening and talking is only part of the job. Actually, it's useless to have conversations without taking action about stakeholders' issues, concerns, and expectations. Communication is an active, iterative, and progressive effort.

To be objective and clear when communicating is crucial to avoid misunderstandings, but we can't forget about rapport and kindness when dealing with people. Stakeholders are a special type of people in projects because they are affected, or they can influence the results of the project. In a way, we could think of them as allies and enemies of the project objectives.

Because of that, stakeholder identification is extremely important. Once identified, it is time to get in touch with them to show our good intentions. Here we employ our selling and psychological knowledge to help us in getting buy-in. We want more than simple agreement, we want involvement and support from stakeholders. The more engaged they are, the better for the project because we can make early corrections as necessary.

If stakeholders' satisfaction is a measure of success in projects, they have to be tightly involved in requirements and scope definition. But satisfaction is not only about the project's results, it is also a result of relationships.

Have you ever gone into a restaurant or a hotel with great food and accommodations? Were you ever treated unkindly? If so, your experience and satisfaction were not good. Even when we get the best product with low cost and time, if we are not treated respectfully, we won't be satisfied.

In project management, the relationship factor is more important because of duration. A two-year project demands building a lasting relationship with stakeholders. In addition, considering that modern stakeholders are more sophisticated, they want more information about the ongoing project and they want to influence it more. That's our new biggest challenge as project managers.

Even if we control technology or if we are proficient in project management, the purpose of a project is strictly related to stakeholders' ownership. Doing the right projects is more important than simply doing projects right. A big consequence is that project managers now have to behave like consultants and teachers, adapting their approaches as they interact with stakeholders.

We could say that project management is not about descriptive methods nor about well-structured methodologies; it is a learning process that involves stakeholders in a constructive endeavor. Because of that, communication is paramount. The project manager's job is to understand stakeholders, to show tradeoffs, to sell benefits of possible solutions, while being honest and focused on the objective of the project.

12.3 Essential Stakeholder Management

Stakeholder management deals with interests, influence and impact of stakeholders. The first obvious step is stakeholder identification: whoever affects or is affected by the project. As long as we have a list of stakeholders, we can gather information about their interests: what are the expectations of stakeholders? Stakeholder analysis also identifies their influence: legitimate authority that stakeholders have in the project and "commodities" (sources) of power. Further, assessing stakeholders' impact helps in defining stakeholder management strategies by prioritizing action plans based in stakeholders' importance to the project.

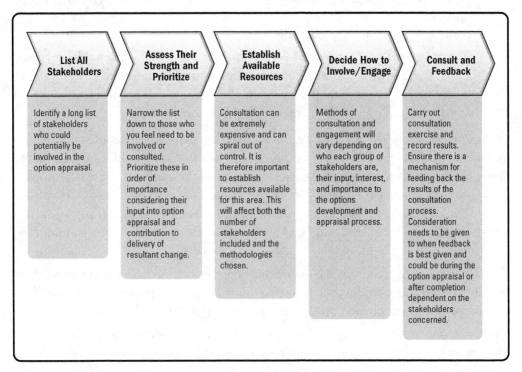

Figure 12-1: Essential stakeholder management steps.

In summary, we have four essential processes in project stakeholder management. No matter in what order, they have to be part of every project management methodology:

1) Identify Stakeholders

The process of identifying all relevant people or organizations impacted by the project, analyzing and documenting relevant information regarding their interests, involvement, interdependencies, and potential impact on project success. Don't forget to prioritize stakeholders and common issues.

2) Plan Stakeholder Management

The process of developing appropriate management strategies to effectively engage stakeholders in project decisions and execution based on the analysis of their needs, interests, and potential impact. Remember the law of diminishing returns and focus on rational resource allocation balancing the cost/benefit relation of managing stakeholders.

3) Manage Stakeholder Engagement

The process of communicating and working with stakeholders to meet their needs/expectations, address issues as they occur, and foster appropriate stakeholder engagement in project decisions and activities. A good plan with poor implementation will not give you any competitive advantage in managing projects.

4) Control Stakeholder Engagement

The process of monitoring and controlling overall project stakeholder relationships and adjusting strategies and plans for engaging stakeholders. Stakeholder management is an iterative ongoing cycle, which implies feedback and adjustments like in a PDCA cycle (Plan-Do-Check-Act).

It's obvious that we need processes to identify, plan, and execute stakeholder management. But why do we have a process to monitor stakeholder management? Well, as projects pick up momentum, your ability to remember details quickly falls away because of the volume of information. On the other hand, we already know that stakeholders are so important to projects that you can't afford to forget them that's why monitoring and controlling these relationships cannot be overlooked.

The process of monitoring stakeholder engagement has to be structured. It is useful to develop tools to do that. You can use from simple spreadsheets to sophisticated customer relationship management software (CRM).

It is crucial to conduct periodical satisfaction assessments of key stakeholders. You can create questionnaires for different types or categories of stakeholders to get a total score of important aspects for each.

Table 12-1: Example of stakeholder engagement assessment scores.

Stakeholder Engagement Assessment (or Satisfaction Assessment)	Score
Contractors and Suppliers	
Commitment (PM scores)	3
Involvement in Planning (PM scores)	3
Communication	4
Conflicts management	4
Sponsor	
Motivation (PM scores)	2
Commitment (PM scores)	2
Communication	3
Other Key Stakeholders	
Organizational Culture (PM scores)	3
Commitment (PM scores)	3
Alignment	3
Communication	4
Perceived Value	4
Team Members	
Motivation (PM scores)	4
Commitment (PM scores)	4
Job satisfaction	3
Conflicts management	4
Communication	5
Skills	3

Score	Criteria
0	Nothing done, no results, no process in place
1	Work started, but major improvement required
2	Some work done, still in progress and behind expectations
3	Meets requirements and expectations, no significant problems
4	Above average results and process in place, well managed and executed

In Table 12-1, we have some aspects that are scored by stakeholders and some scored by the project manager considering what he or she feels from stakeholders. It is important to elaborate better questions to assess stakeholder engagement and satisfaction; the previous figure is very simplified.

So, we have two ways to execute these types assessments, and we can merge them. The first approach is that the project manager can ask stakeholders to give a score for every important aspect related to their group. However, sometimes it's better, or easier, when the project manager does (or delegates) this assessment. In this case, the project manager would score the important aspects for each key stakeholder, based on what is observed in his or her relationship with them.

Englund and Bucero (2006) say that it is important to have a feedback action plan to help in stakeholder management.

Table 12-2: Feedback action plan (*Project Sponsorship*, Englund & Bucero, 2006, p. 129 Used with permission.).

Data Collected	Time	Media	Timing of Feedback	Action Required
1. Previous project survey	Beginning of the project	Meeting, survey summary	Kick-off meeting, planned meeting	Adjust actions or approach
2. Project implementation survey	Beginning of the implementation	Survey		Adjust approach
3. Interviews or approach	One month later	Meeting	Meeting date	Adjust actions
4. Project implementation feedback or survey	End of implementation	Survey	Project implementation review	Adjust actions or approach

12.4 People-oriented

In previous chapters, I've stressed the role of project managers as leaders, motivating and inspiring to get buy-in for the project. Leaders use power and politics to accomplish the vision they cast for the project with the help of key stakeholders. On the other hand, it is not possible to be a good leader without managerial skills. Managers are known for being task oriented and concerned with satisfying stakeholders by delivering results that meet their needs.

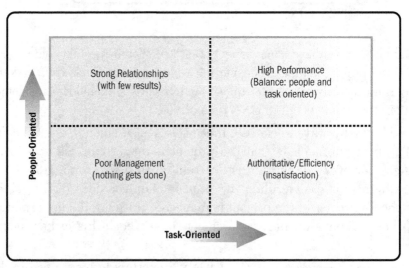

Figure 12-2: People- and task-oriented approaches.

Reward and punishment, derived from the power and authority, are tools that the project manager has to know how to use wisely. When dealing with people, rationality is blurred by emotions. In particular, team management is not easy.

If you have more than one person working on your project, you have a team, which means a wide assortment of personalities, skills, and needs. As a project manager, you'll have to manage your team members at the same time you are dealing with other project stakeholders. Usually, there will be a lot of different viewpoints and conflicting interests.

Some of these conflicts will affect the performance of the project team. For example, loyalty to functional managers and part-time team members create issues that the project manager has to address properly. We've already been through that.

But how can we connect with people? Appelo (2010) dedicated part of his book stressing the importance of connecting with people, and he gave us some tips and examples on how to do that. Creating and maintaining meaningful connections with stakeholders is not only nice; it is a cornerstone to the system (organization or project) as a whole.

Good relationships improve resilience and also provide better communications and enhance creativity because people are willing to contribute. There are no half-cooked recipes to do that. The advice is to fail fast and learn. Again, feedback is critical. Focus on getting feedback from stakeholders, and you'll learn and adjust your strategy to connect with them in favor of your project.

Project managers need to concentrate more on managing the front end, which means they have to be involved with the project on an operational level, managing the interaction between the project and its environment. Project managers organize and manage interfaces with stakeholders to best meet project objectives. A special group of stakeholders are the team members.

Appelo (2010) says that high-performing teams are ones who regularly submit their work to each other to improve it. There is more collaboration and less competition. This *esprit de corps* is constructed during team building. Also, in this environment, there is more tolerance, no one is expected to get the work right the first time and on one's own (Appelo, 2011).

Excellent results come from peer reviews, driven by a shared value of accountability for the success of the team, project, or organization (Appelo, 2011). And how do we, project managers, create such an environment? We are directive leaders who set the goals and the boundaries so that the group can become a team on their own, by establishing ground rules and by evolving through Tuckman's (1965) stages of team building. Remember that we are dealing with knowledge workers and they have higher levels of maturity, which implies that we orient them and delegate responsibilities.

Communication is an important pillar to achieve higher team performance. While it is important to give and take feedback on personal and team behaviors, it is also important to communicate achieved project results to interested stakeholders. Feedback throughout the project ensures that information is flowing so that changes or adjustments can be made to achieve project success. In summary, there are two main roles for communication in projects: feedback from and to stakeholder and project information dissemination.

Remember also that the project manager is the focal point; he or she concentrates on guidance and directions for the project. Consequently, the project manager has to be recognized and act as the formal information source of the project. Project managers have to actively look for communication opportunities, uncovering and making clear the project objectives, roles, and responsibilities. Being transparent and coherent is extremely important to establish and enforce credibility.

Be aware that project management goes beyond techniques to complete projects on time, scope, and budget. It is about creating enterprise value (Office of Government Commerce, 2009; Project Management Institute, 2008). Improving organizational performance depends on getting more accomplished through projects because they make the strategy happen.

But, and that's a big but, no amount of team building or stakeholder management will make up for poor project planning or ineffective project management techniques. Managing projects are not only about people, it is also about knowledge and techniques. Neglecting these things will cost you big failures in projects.

12.5 Knowledge Management

Why is it so difficult to conduct good lessons learned sessions? Why is knowledge management usually ineffective? Well, many people are reactive and afraid of controls. Documenting what you have done brings responsibilities because papers can be audited in the future. Besides, they can be used to evaluate an employee's performance.

One common error is to collect lessons learned only at the end of the project. You and your team will probably have forgotten much of the details and issues. Lessons learned should be conducted periodically as a tool to improve the project itself and future projects.

Appelo (2010) said that error, whether random or deliberate, must become an integral part of any process of creation. Learning can be thought of as systematic error management. That's why he recommended the use of regular retrospectives to discuss the current situation and how to improve on it. So, lessons learned are not only about adaptation (responding to issues or problems), but also about exploration and anticipation, which leads us to continuous improvement.

Many project managers and their organizations need to manage knowledge and to keep historical records. However, by not taking the right time to analyze past results and issues during the project life cycle, organizations commonly lose great learning and improvement opportunities.

Englund and Bucero (2006) recommended implementing "project snapshots," half-day sessions whose purpose is to capture lessons learned during a project, preserve knowledge for reuse, and identify opportunities for skill or methodology improvement for all project stakeholders. Englund and Bucero (2006) say that the objectives for these sessions are as follows:

- To reflect on successes and lessons learned in project selling and implementation phases;
- To focus around key themes such as project and scope management, communication, issue management, problems, and successes;
- To leverage successes and learning to more effectively deliver subsequent phases or projects for clients; and
- To identify tools and best practices that can be shared more broadly.

In particular, we use a similar approach, as proposed by Englund and Bucero (2006), at the Institute of Aeronautics and Space, which resulted in great benefits. Here we have not only periodical lessons learned sessions conducted by the project managers but also periodical presentations done by project managers to all stakeholders and employees about progress, status, issues, and lessons learned of projects. Everybody in the organization has access, or the opportunity, to know what is going on in other projects and to discuss their lessons learned together.

Lessons learned sessions are the best way of knowledge management. People felt more comfortable discussing problems and lessons learned than when they are writing reports. Usually, documented lessons learned are not consulted because time urges project managers to rush on project planning and execution without much time to research the organizational process assets. Knowledge transmission by experience exchanges is a very powerful tool that should be stimulated.

Besides lessons learned sessions, we usually have review sessions that are more related to status meetings. They are used to monitor and control the project results as well as to inform stakeholders.

Englund and Bucero (2006) noted the advantages of these review sessions and lessons learned sessions: they generate value for the professionals, for the project team, for the project manager, for the project sponsor, and for the rest of the organization. For professionals, the sessions leverage team members' work and experience through sharing lessons learned, prevent redundant activities by having all team members understand what each person has worked on and is working on. They resolve issues earlier in the project by getting them surfaced and resolved. For the project team, the sessions leverage learning and successes for ongoing project work deliver a more consistent implementation by having everyone on the project get better aligned.

People are creative only when they feel it is safe to express their ideas. That's why team building, trust, and open communications are so important, not only in executing the project but also in gathering lessons learned. Feeling safe means not being afraid to express ideas and ask questions.

Bibliography

Appelo, J. (2010). *Management 3.0*. Boston, MA: Addison-Wesley.

Blanchard, B. S. (2008). *Systems engineering management*. 4th edition. New York. John Wiley & Sons.

Bryson, J. M. (2004). What to do when stakeholders matter: Stakeholder identification and analysis techniques. *Public Management Review 6*(1), 21–53.

Bryson, J. M., Patton, M. Q., & Bowman, R. A. (2011). *Working with evaluation stakeholders: A rationale, step-wise approach and toolkit*. Evaluation and Program Planning 34 (2011) 1–12, DOI:10.1016/j.evalprogplan.2010.07.001

Cabanis, J., & Paul, C. D. (2006). *The AMA handbook of project management*. 2nd ed. New York: AMACOM.

Carpinetti, L., Mateus G., & Paulo M. (2009). *Gestão da Qualidade ISO 9001:2008: Princípios e Requisitos*. Ed. Atlas.

Carvalho, M. M., & Rabechini, R. (2008). *Construindo Competências para Gerenciar Projetos: Teoria e Casos*. Ed. Atlas.

Carnegie, D. (2004). *How to stop worrying and start living*. New York: Simon & Schuster.

Carnegie, D. (2009). *How to win friends and influence people*. New York: Gallery Books.

Carroll, L. (1998). *Alice's adventures in wonderland and through the looking-glass*. London, UK: Penguin Classics.

Checkland, P. (1975). The origins and nature of "hard systems" thinking. *Journal of Applied Systems Analysis 5*(2): 99–110.

Checkland, P. (1981). *Systems thinking, systems practice*. London: Wiley.

Checkland, P., & Winter, M. (2005). Process and content: Two ways of using SSM. *Journal of the Operational Research Society 57*(12): 1435–1441.

Checkland, P., & Scholes, J. (1999). *Soft systems methodology: A 30-year retrospective*. 1st ed. Chichester, UK: John Wiley.

Christensen, C. M. (1997). *The innovator's dilemma: When technologies cause great firms to fail*. Boston, MA: Harvard Business School Press.

Cleland, D., ed. (2004). *Field guide to project management*. 2nd ed. New York: John Wiley & Sons.

Cleland, D., & Ireland L., eds. (2008). *Project manager's handbook: Applying best practices across global industries*. New York: McGraw Hill.

Cohn, M. (2005). *Agile estimating and planning*. Houston: Prentice Hall.

Cohn, M. (2009). *Succeeding with agile: Software development using scrum.* New York: Addison-Wesley.

Cooper, D., Grey, S., Raymond, G., & Walker, P. (2005). *Project risk management guidelines: Managing risk in large projects and complex procurements.* Chichester, UK: John Wiley & Sons.

Covey, S. (2004). *The 7 habits of highly effective people.* New York: Free Press.

Davis, J., Macdonald, A., & White, L. (2010). Problem-structuring methods and project management: An example of stakeholder involvement using Hierarchical Process Modelling methodology. *Journal of Operational Research Society 61*(6), 893–904.

Department of Defense. (1991). *Draft DOD Software Technology Strategy.* Washington, DC: Director of Defense Research and Engineering. Retrieved from www.dod.gov/pubs/logistics_material_readiness

Defense Acquisition University. n.d. Retrieved from https://acc.dau.mil/docs/technicalreviews/dod_tech_reviews.htm

Defense Acquisition University. Concept of Operations Template. Retrieved from https://acc.dau.mil/CommunityBrowser.aspx?id=245888

Defense Acquisition University. (2001). *Systems engineering fundamentals.* Fort Belvoir: DAU University Press.

Drucker, P. F. (2008). *The essential of Drucker: The best of sixty years of Peter Drucker's essential writings on management.* New York: Collins Business Essentials.

Englund, R. L., & Alfonso, B. (2006). *Project sponsorship: Achieving management commitment for project success.* San Francisco: Jossey-Bass.

Englund, R. L., Graham, R., & Dinsmore, P. C. (2003). *Creating the project office: A manager's guide to leading organizational change.* San Francisco: Jossey-Bass.

Ferraro, J. (2008). *The strategic project leader.* New York: Auerbach.

Finkelstein, S., Campbell, A., & Whitehead, J. (2009). *Think again: Why good leaders make bad decisions and how to keep it from happening to you.* Boston, MA: Harvard Business School Press.

Flanes, S. W., & Levin, G. (2001). *People skills for project managers.* Vienna: Management Concepts.

Gardiner, P. D. (2005). *Project management.* New York: Palgrave Macmillan.

Goleman, D. (2006). *Emotional intelligence: Why it can matter more than IQ, 10th Anniversary Edition.* New York: Bantam.

Gladwell, M. (2002). *The tipping point.* Boston: Back Bay Books.

Gladwell, M. (2007). *The tipping point.* Boston: Back Bay Books.

Hartman, F. T. (2000). *Don't park your brain outside: A practical guide to improving shareholder value with smart management.* 1st ed. Newtown Square, PA: Project Management Institute.

Hersey, P., & Blanchard, K. H. (1977). *Management of organizational behavior: Utilizing human resources.* 3rd ed. Upper Saddle River, NJ: Prentice Hall.

Howick, S., & Eden, C. (2001). The impact of disruption and delay when compressing large projects: Going for incentives? *Journal of the Operational Research Society* 52(1): 26–34.

Howick, S., & Eden, C. (2007). Learning in disrupted projects: On the nature of corporate and personal learning. *International Journal of Production Research* 45(12): 2775–2797.

Hubbard, D. W. (2010). *How to measure anything: Finding the value of intangibles in business.* Hoboken, NJ: John Wiley & Sons.

Hubbard, D. W. (2009). *The failure of risk management: Why it's broken and how to fix it.* Hoboken, New Jersey: John Wiley & Sons.

Hull, E., Jackson, K., & Dick, J. (2011). *Requirements engineering, 3rd edition.* London, UK: Springer.

Hunter, J. (1998). *The servant: A simple story about the true essense of leadership.* Prima.

IT Cortex. Project Failure Causes: Statistics. n.d. Retrieved from www.it-cortex.com/stat_failure_cause.htm,.

International Organization for Standardization. (2008). ISO 15288: *Systems and Software Engineering: System Life Cycle Processes.*

Kano, N. (1984). Attractive quality and must-be quality. *Journal of the Japanese Society for Quality Control,* April, 39–48.

Kerzner, H. (2006). *Gestão de Projetos: As melhores práticas.* Ed. Bookman.

Kerzner, H. (2001). *Strategic planning for project management using a project management maturity model.* New York: John Wiley & Sons.

Kerzner, H. (2009) *Project management,.* 10th ed. Hoboken, NJ: John Wiley & Sons.

Kerzner, H. (2011). Project management metrics, KPIs, and dashboard: A guide to measuring and monitoring project performance. New York: International Institute for Learning Inc.

Kerzner, H. (1992). *Project management: A systems approach to planning, scheduling and controlling.* New York: Van Nostrand Reinhold.

Kouzes, J. M., & Posner, B. Z. (1993). *Credibility: How leaders gain and lose it, why people demand it.* San Francisco: Jossey-Bass.

Larman, C., & Bas Vodde. (2009). *Scaling lean and agile development: Thinking and organizational tools for large-scale scrum.* London: Addison-Wesley.

Lewis, J. P. (2000). *The project manager's desk reference.* 2nd ed. Boston: McGraw-Hill.

Macedo, O., Vivacqua, F., & Xavier, C. M. (2009). *Metodologia de Gerenciamento de Projetos: Methodware.* 3a. Edição. Editora Brasport.

Mai, R., & Akerson, A. (2003). *The leader as a communicator.* New York: AMACOM.

Maximiniano, A. (2008). *Administração de Projetos: Como transformar ideias em resultados*. São Paulo: Atlas.

Meredith, J., & Mantel, Jf. S. J. (2000). *Project management: A managerial approach*. New York: Wiley.

Mersino, A. (2007). *Emotional intelligence for project managers: The people skills you need to achieve outstanding results*. New York: Amacom.

Mitchell, R. K., Agle, B. R., & Wood, D. J. (1997). Toward a theory of stakeholder identification and salience: Defining the principle of who and what really counts. *Academy of Management Review 22*(4): 853–886.

Mintzberg, H. (2009). *Managing*. San Francisco: Ignatius Press.

Monteleone, M. A. (2010). *"Generic questions for interviewing stakeholders."* Business Analyst Times, Retrieved from http://www.batimes.com/articles/generice-questions-for-interviewing-stakeholders.html.

Mountain Goat Software. (n.d.) Retrieved from www.mountaingoatsoftware.com

Mulcahy, R. (2009). *PMP exam prep. 6th edition*. RMC Publications.

Mulcahy, R. (2003). *Risk management: Tricks of the trade for project managers*. RMC Publications.

National Aeronautics and Space Administration. (2005). *Systems Engineering Handbook*. NASA PPMI: Washington, DC.

Office of Government Commerce. (2009). *An introduction to PRINCE2: Managing and directing successful projects*. London: The Stationary Office.

Office of Government Commerce. (2009). *Directing successful projects with PRINCE2*. London: The Stationary Office.

Office of Government Commerce. (2009). *Managing successful projects with PRINCE2*. London: The Stationary Office.

Office of Government Commerce. (2009). *Portfolio, programme and project offices: P3O*. London: The Stationary Office.

Phillips, J. (2009). *PgMP® Program Management Professional: Exam Guide*. New York: McGraw-Hill.

Pink, D. (2011). *Drive, the surprising truth about what motivates us*. New York: Penguin Group.

Harari, O. (2004). *The Powell principles: 24 lessons from Colin Powell, a battle-proven leader*. New York: McGraw-Hill.

Pryor, K. (2006). *Don't shoot the dog: The new art of teaching and training*. Ringpress Books.

Project Management Institute. (2008). *A guide to the project management body of knowledge (PMBOK® Guide)*—4th ed. Newtown Square, PA: Author.

Project Management Institute. (2008). *Organizational project management maturity model (OPM3®)*—2nd ed. Newtown Square, PA: Author.

Project Management Institute. (2011). *Practice standard for earned value management*—2nd ed. Newtown Square, PA: Author.

Project Management Institute. (2009). *Practice standard for project risk management*. Newtown Square, PA: Author.

Project Management Institute. (2011). *Practice standard for scheduling*—2nd ed. Newtown Square, PA: Author.

Project Management Institute. (2011). *Practice standard for work breakdown structures*—2nd ed. Newtown Square, PA: Author.

Project Management Institute. (2008). *The standard for portfolio management*—2nd ed. Newtown Square, PA: Author.

Project Management Institute. (2008). *The standard for program management*—2nd ed. Newtown Square, PA: Author.

Shenhar, A. J., & Dvir, D. (2007). *Reinventing project management: The diamond approach to successful growth and innovation*. Boston, MA: Harvard Business School Press.

Sun T. (2009). *The art of war*. London: Penguin Classics.

Rackham, N. (1988). *SPIN selling*. New York: McGraw-Hill.

Schwaber, K. (2004). *Agile project management with scrum*. New York: Microsoft Press.

Schwaber, K. (2007). *The enterprise and scrum*. New York: Microsoft Press.

Schwartz, B. (2005). *The paradox of choice: Why more is less*. New York: Harper Perennial.

Senge, P. (2006). *The fifth discipline*. San Francisco: Ignatius Press.

Stacey, R. D., et.al. (2000). *Complexity and management*. New York: Routledge.

Stewart, W. M., & Sheremeta, P. W. (2000). *Will you be terminated today*. Houston: Project Management Institute Global Congress 2000.

Thull, J. (2007). Gestão de vendas complexas. São Paulo: Campus.

Thull, J. (2010). Mastering the complex sale. New York: John Wiley & Sons.

Trentim, M. H. (2011). *Gerenciamento de projetos: Guia para as certificações CAPM e PMP*. São Paulo: Atlas.

Trentim, M. H. (2012). *Manual do MS-Project 2010 e Melhores Práticas do PMI*. São Paulo: Atlas.

Trentim, M. H., & Mariana, G. L. (2010). *Gerenciamento de stakeholders: Case BP no Golfo do México*. Revista Mundo PM 34 (Agosto).

Tuckman, B. (1965). Developmental sequence in small groups. *Psychological Bulletin*, Vol. 63, 384–399.

Tuckman, B. (1977). Stages of small group development revisited. London: *Group & Organization Studies 2*(4), 419–427.

Vargas, R. V. (2009). *Gerenciamento de projetos*. 7a. Edição. Ed. Brasport.

Vargas, R. V. (2009). *Manual prático de planejamento de projeto*. Ed. Brasport.

Vargas, R. V. (2004). *Using earned value management indexes as a team development factor and a compensation tool*. Prague: Project Management Institute Global Congress EMEA.

Walton, M. S. (2004). *Generating buy-in: Mastering the language of leadership.* New York: AMACOM.

Wideman, R. M. (2004). "How to motivate all stakeholders to work together." In *Field Guide to Project Management,* edited by D. I. Cleland, 288–304. 2nd ed. New York: John Wiley & Sons.

Winter, M. (2006). Problem structuring in project management: An application. *J Opl Res Soc 57*(7): 802–812.

Winter, M., & Checkland, P. (2003). Soft systems: A fresh perspective for project management. *P I Civil Eng Civ Eng 156*(4): 187–192.

Young, R. (2004). *Requirements engineering handbook.* Norwood, MA: Artech House.